Changing Harm
to Harmony

Changing Harm to Harmony

Bullies & Bystanders Project

A Book of Poems, Letters
& Other Writings

Edited by Joseph Zaccardi

Poet Laureate of Marin County, California

MARIN
POETRY
CENTER

ISBN: 978-0-9762478-3-8
Book and cover design by Jeremy Thornton, jftdesign.com
Cover art and frontispiece monoprint, *Alone*.
Copyright © 2013 by Richard Cruwys Brown.

Grateful acknowledgment is made to the Marin County Free Library System for
their support for the Marin County Poet Laureate program and the Bullies and
Bystanders project.

**MARIN
POETRY
CENTER**

Marin Poetry Center Press
PO Box 9091
San Rafael, CA 94912

in memoriam
Patrick Smith

———•———

9.7.1931 – 10.9.2013

CONTENTS

Introduction

Being a lover of words, the idea of changing *harm* to *harmony* has always intrigued me. When I began this project I looked up the etymology of both words, because I thought there must be an association. *Harm,* of course, is in opposition to *harmony.* I learned *harm* comes to us from the Old English, meaning *grief, sorrow,* and *physical injury,* while *harmony,* a much older word, comes from Latin, meaning *a joining.* My goal then was to find a way to change what I believe is harmful to both perpetrator and victim; to bring about a harmonious interaction between two words whose meanings have no basis for comparison. As one questioner asked, "I wonder how you're going to do that?" But I was convinced that between the hurtfulness of *harm* and the helpfulness of *harmony,* poets and writers could find a way to reconcile the disharmony.

The first question asked of me when I proposed a book of poems, letters and other writings on the theme of bullies and bystanders, was, why poetry? Fair enough. I explained a poem can touch one in a way that is easily remembered, whereas a novel like *Lord of the Flies,* or the movies *Boys Don't Cry* and *Pay It Forward,* can and do change the way people think about social issues. However, they aren't something that can easily be shared with others without a person having read that same book or watched those same films. Poems, on the other hand, can be carried under the breastbone and recited by heart.

With the addition of letters and other writings, my hope was to include readers and writers who may be put-off by poetry. All persons, even if they struggle with its composition, can write a letter about experiences or feelings, because a letter allows one the freedom to juggle syntax, misspell a word, make those wonderful run-on sentences, and/or jump from one subject to another without seeming odd. In this way the letter is like a poem, a dramatic monologue if you will, where the recipients can feel for themselves and respond to the senders.

Here is an example of a letter and three retellings of real-life incidents:

Dear L,

You remember the peach and plum trees we planted together last fall, they are not without an owner. My old rustic wall may be low, but this is still a private home. It is just like a bully to come in the night and break several blossoming branches, to destroy something of beauty for no reason other than to cause harm. Now I no longer have solace.

Come visit me again. Won't you?

Sincerely, D

This is actually a poem by Du Fu, a Tang dynasty poet, composed in 761 C.E., addressed to his close friend, Li Bai. Of course it was translated without any of the rhyme the poem originally had, and I got rid of the anglicized line breaks, put it into a more prose-like style, added a greeting and salutation, and *voilà*, it becomes a letter. And this reminds me of what the poet and novelist Michael Ondaatje wrote, and I paraphrase, "The postcard is the American sonnet." I think we all have had thoughts that are poetic and write them down and send them off to friends.

What can a bystander do? I have two personal experiences, and one from a friend, that I'd like to share. The first event took place when I was 13 years old, in the play yard at St. Mary's primary school during recess. Six kids were picking on a classmate who was very obese. These kids were taking turns punching him in the stomach. Because of his physical condition he couldn't run away. I don't know what possessed me to step in between them or where I found the courage to do this, often being bullied myself, but I stood in front of Richard, my arms outstretched, and said to these kids, "Leave him alone, hit me instead."

What happened was their leader gave us a disgusted look and said some-thing like, "Ah, forget them." I'm not suggesting that this was very wise, things could have turned out badly, but what I learned that day was that a bystander could make a difference.

Here is a second example of how a poem can make a difference: a teacher from a local high school submitted a packet of poems from her students on the theme of bullies and bystanders. As I was going through them I came across a poem that was a desperate cry for help. The young poet described how she was belittled and berated in her home and how at school, obviously not in the presence of adults, she was verbally abused and humiliated. She wrote that she would go into the bathroom and look in the mirror and talk to herself; she wrote that she was afraid she would "hurt herself"; one stand-alone line said, "Help Me." As you can imagine I was beside myself. I called a friend and he said I should call the school authorities immediately. I did and was quickly put through to this youngster's teacher, and she in turn contacted the school coun-selor, who assured me in a follow-up phone call that they would get on this right away. I related this episode only a few weeks later, at a panel discussion on bullying. One of the panelists brought to my attention the fact that a poem can be written in privacy and turned over to someone who would listen and do something.

And thirdly, and this was an eye-opener for me, was a conversation I had with a poet/friend of mine whom I've known for twenty years, who told me she was a bully in high school. Her story surprised me because she's beautiful, intelligent, and generous. I remember saying, "You!" She explained that her father was a garbage man, nowadays called a sanitation worker. You can see that this could and did lead to some nasty remarks by her peers. To compensate, she ridiculed another girl who had acne. She said that this made her feel good, and that further-more she didn't think it did any harm; after all it was just verbal abuse. About three months later we met again for lunch and she said she was able to track down the woman she had bullied, who happened to still live in the same town she grew up in, in rural Washington State. My friend was stunned that this former classmate remembered her taunts and that she still felt the sting and hurt. A long conversation ensued, ending with both of them in tears. Things were patched up and plans were made to meet: a joining, a time to forgive, a time to change *harm* to *harmony*.

Now here's how I came to the decision of how to define bullying and set the parameters for this book, because this subject encompasses physical and verbal abuse, racial prejudice, sexual abuse of children and adults, cyber bullying, and a whole range of other things, including intimidation in our schools, the workplace, and the home. One could even draw an arc to Nazism and terrorism. As a starting point I made the decision to limit the scope to things that were not already treated as crimes. But as the submissions came in, it became clear to me that I had to allow some leeway in this self-imposed confine. So here and there you will find writings that blur the line. I also felt compelled to present contradictory ideas. I was inspired to take this route when I heard Wendell Berry, the poet and philosopher, speak on a Bill Moyers program about the environmental disrepair of the earth, and I paraphrase again, "If you think there is only one answer, than you are implying that there is only one question." I feel that this applies to bullies and bystanders. This is what I asked myself about each submission that crossed my desk, allowing for different points of view (even ones that I don't agree with), and different questions and answers. Maybe someday soon, a Norton-style anthology of nine hundred pages, a door-stopper for sure, will be made available on this subject, and perhaps some of the material from *Changing Harm to Harmony* will be included. And perhaps each little piece put together from many sources will help make a difference.

Lastly, and most importantly, this book of poems and letters grew out of the fine writing I received, and from the compassion of the authors from all walks of life, from a wide range of age groups and backgrounds. It now takes this form because of the commitment and craft of the poets and writers herein. I thank you all. And to those who took the time to read and advise, and there were many, I thank you also. And to the people I didn't know, who I approached at the Café Aroma, in San Rafael, California, who didn't think it strange that I came to their tables proffering creased pages of poems, letters and other writings, asking them to read something important and give me their opinions, I am deeply indebted and humbled.

— Joseph Zaccardi

Looked at Him

In high school he picked a fight with a kid he knew he could beat. What had the kid done? Not a thing. *Looked at him.*

They met in the back lot when school let out. Big crowd. It was quick. This to show his friends, of course. Blood on the kid's mouth.

As years went by he thought back on that scene, and when he did, he felt like shit. It wore on him.

He paid a clerk in his law firm to look him up. The man had moved to upstate New York.

Wrote him a note: "Not a year has gone by I have not thought of that day. It makes me feel so bad." When he sent off the note, he felt a great weight lift.

Two weeks passed, then came the man's note.

"I see that you have not changed a bit."

{Gerald Fleming lives in Lagunitas, California. Born and raised in San Francisco, California. Poet & Teacher.}

Such a Pretty Face

The aunties lean in clucking, a barnyard
        of hens, better, a stewpot of them.
The aunties pinching your cheeks like Granny
        testing the plucked chicken.
The aunties, their eyes moving down your body
        as if assessing Clementina, the Flying Pig.
Boys on the corner, pointing like Uncle Sam posters
        making a loud chorus of oink sounds.
Boys in the school yard with grimy hands
        playing push you, pull you, shove you over.
Girls in their Barbie Doll sweater sets, with their
        whispers like the monsters under the bed.
Construction guys across the street whistling
        like mocking birds.
Grandmother taking you to the lingerie department
        and snorting, like a sow rejecting the slops.
The aunties singing of their daughters, Loreleis
        on a river bank.
The aunties whispering to Mother, like leaves in a wind.
Great Grandmother moving her antique chair
        like an auctioneer gauging value.
The swimsuit saleslady, always across the room,
        as if a barrier had risen.
Uncle Bob grabbing your thigh as if he's kneading breast.
Uncle Bob mouthing off like a gibbon in a tree.
Mother serving a smaller portion like a family in poverty.
Janie refusing to loan you her sweater like a dog in the manger.
Grandmother opening her arms, happy to see you, saying,
        "So sad. Such a pretty face."

———————————————

———⋙◆⋘———

"Such a Pretty Face" was written from some experiences I've had as an adult, and some experiences I can imagine an overweight child feeling. As a really skinny kid, and quite skinny thru college, my mother was constantly urging me TO EAT. I was also very athletic. Won the Women's Athlete Cup my senior year etc., was on all my high school and college teams. It was really when all that activity stopped, except for weekly tennis, say, that things got out of hand, that is, my weight gain.

I actually wrote this poem for the Bullies and Bystanders Panel Discussion, at Falkirk Cultural Center in San Rafael, California, back on November 2013. As one of the panelist I got to thinking about the bullying that our parents, families etc. inflict on their kids, even on kids who don't seem to have issues inviting bullying. It so often starts with the parents. I think they over-want their kids to be perfect, or want to find fault because they are worried, or need to be in control, or need to pick on others because of how they feel about themselves. Sometimes consciously, sometimes unconsciously.

We need to be more aware as humans but especially as parents of the lasting impacts of our words and actions, negative and also positive. Compassion, that's a great word to keep in mind.

{CB Follett lives in Sausalito, California. Born in NYC, raised in Connecticut. Poet & General Dogsbody. arctospress.com}

Image

Image, I define you, as wretched and counterfeit;
I look time and time again, only to see what I can't get.
Image, you defy me, as brutal, and loathsome abound;
I wake to find, something great, but gasps be my only sound.
I loath you image, flawed and gross, always too this and too that;
No, I mean I loath myself, not pretty and much too fat.
Image, I worship you, through starvation and retching to nil;
I seek to see myself in you, at the risk of becoming dark and still.
Image, I adore you, for I have suffered you to bleak;
I look to be, all I see, and be all that you seek.
Image, I admire you greatly, and willing to do the work;
As I empty gut and soul, on knees bent low to jerk.
Image, I abandon you, no longer enslaved, betrayed;
Inward try, and outward cry, to crave and crave, be brave.
Image, you are dread to me and now curse me hate and loath;
I put you down to death by sea, and whisk you out like foam.
Image, I control you now, and nurture the beauty found;
I am light, and free, and shine, to wear again my nature's crown!

{L. King Dutton lives in Decatur, Alabama. Born in New Smyrna, Florida. Survivor & Believer.}

Being Primate

First, understand
your forest, tree, water,
who is sharing your space,
what they want from you. Imagine
that you are orangutan, gorilla, chimpanzee,
or simply human.
The code among cells is not so different
yet in that difference, a chasm,
and in that chasm,
extinction.

Even among your own species,
you are sometimes regarded
as if you are in the wrong
forest, tree, or house,
as if your skin and hair are detestable,
your customs, incomprehensible,
your clothing, an affront,
as if you are a problem
that requires an immediate solution.

And when they solve the problem
that is you, when you have been reduced
to that most common denominator, dust,
there are no more codes or cells.
Others come and live where you once lived.
You are so closely related,
you are family.

{Margaret Stawowy lives in Novato, California. Born and raised in
Chicago, Illinois. Librarian & Poet.}

Fat Kid

Three hundred pounds in seventh grade and growing,
fattest kid in school, Sid in the horn section
nearly blocked my view of our director
from where I labored, back row, on tenor sax.
I could see his neck going pink, sweat slipping
down Dizzy Gillespie cheeks, eyes squinting
as his stubby fingers worked the keys. We lived
two blocks apart. The bus ejected us
at the same stop: slight, skinny me; Big Sid.

That first week of school, we all saw it coming,
and when some tall, long-haired jerk shoved Sidney
in the dirt, a circle rapidly formed
and the coaches vanished like Darwinians
allowing natural selection to run
its course. All Sid could do was raise his fists,
but by then his glasses were broken, and he
was bleeding, and crying, and the crowd jeering.
Tears stung my eyes, but I let no one see them.

After that single, vicious beating, some kind
of equilibrium had been restored,
a necessary order imposed, which all
understood: Sid had to pay for his weight
with a pummeling, it was that simple.
And once endured, he earned a grudging respect;
his tormentor—now that he had filled his function
for us—meanwhile was relegated
to pariah, and dropped out in early Spring.

And so Sidney survived; the taunts continued,
but with lower volume, less frequency.
We learned our instruments, we rode the bus.
His mother, who might have outweighed her son,
kept to the cool back rooms of their dark house.
But she had to be glad to see him with friends,
even ones like me—as I would kid him too,
once in a while—and he would punch me,
hard, in the arm, because it wasn't all right,

and he'd make damned sure at least somebody knew.

The Ropes

The night they tied my brother to a tree,
someone ran to call me from my cabin.
But I got there—as usual—too late;
they'd let him go, and he'd run off to hide,
and cry, not to return until morning.

But I found the tree, around which the kids
in his bunk had danced, and laughed, calling him names
like *Retard! Dummy!* and I found the ropes,
coiled at the base of the tree like snakes.
That summer, we'd learned about tying knots,

and how a tourniquet stops the flow of blood—
except for my brother, who couldn't, was slow,
who to this day can't tie a knot or make
a bow, yet may know as much about them
as any there that night, or anyone not.

{Peter Schmitt lives in Miami, Florida. Creative Writing Teacher & Poet.}

To the Editor: Dear Joe,

Your anthology project will be interesting and so important, particularly because you are including the voices of bystanders as well as the bullied. The story you told of how you were bullied, and yet stood up in front of a heavy boy who was being hit and said "Hit me" stays in my memory. Bullies, I think, are cowards. I am the oldest child of a man who bullied his children (and was bullied by his father), and a protector by nature. It is unendurable for me to see someone picked on, particularly someone who is at a disadvantage. Your story will continue to haunt me. I'm glad you have chosen this project.

rock paper scissors

rock hits scissors
paper smothers rock
words cover paper

scissors stab skin
blood drips on words
rock pities paper

paper hugs rock
scissors free paper
rock sharpens scissors

What a Rock Knows

You had a name like anyone, before
the Haters' Club branded you,
"Dinky Blabber-Mouth." Their chants
shot BBs to your core

of soiled sediment. You were trampled
on a trampoline. Your skin
hardened to stone. Stripped
and stretched apart and locked
outside, you became
a boulder that doesn't budge.

Fossils of your former self
worry into crevices. Your eyes
are chiseled holes that watch
a precipice collapse. The light turns
dark. You can't stop

change. Each day you begin
again like birds sing
to the morning.

{C. Albert resides in Seattle, Washington. Poet & Artist.}

Prosody

Fatso, lard-ass, pig-face, tub

is what they mostly called him
that year he failed P.E.
and religion, — the year
his mother's house burnt down

which was also the year of the flood.

Till then he'd thought of life
as a meaningful motion toward song—.

These days, if you ask him,
he'll just grin, shrug—

say music is as music does.

{Jane Mead lives in Northern California. Teacher & Farmer.}

Not Really a Woman

I am not really a woman
I am a girl
seventeen
curly-haired with too big glasses
awkward and shy

My best friend left me
for another girl, who
was once my friend
We went to the Bronx Zoo and giggled about boys
But later she and my best friend
turned against me

They said
I was staring at them in the senior lounge
They said
I was a sneak
They said
I smelled of the tuna sandwiches I made for the cafeteria

Leave me alone, I wish I had said
Go away
Stop Your Harassment
Now

Two girls against me

They went forward with their lives
and I was left behind
trying to catch up

A girl
seventeen
curly-haired with too big glasses
awkward and shy

{Eva M. Schlesinger lives in Berkeley, California. Born and raised in
Connecticut. Poet & Artist. blogher.com/member/eva-schlesinger}

The Well

I assume
I got it
From you.

My inheritance
Your genes
Your fear.

My habit
Of gritting my jaw
Clenching my face
Into a fist.

A meanness of less
Of no account
Mediocre
Second-rate.

Climbing up the rope
Hand over fist
Out of the well
Exhaustion.

I find you
No longer live here
Still I cower.

Unseen on surface
But sunk inside where
I cannot hide.

Alone

Debased in cyber-techno space
Shifting bits and pieces
Of energy flowing across lines
Without knowing the whole.

In real space machetes and bombs
Rip hearts and minds at a pace
It no longer matters if
The world whimpers to its end.

Yet hawthorn blooms, chickadees sing.
I'm pulled to plant rhododendrons,
Tomatoes, and raspberries as if
There is always a tomorrow.

{MJ Pramik lives in San Francisco, California. Hailing from eastern Ohio's strip mines and hay farmers. Poet & Activist.}

The Invisible Boy

He may get punched once in a while,
but he's usually too invisible
to be picked on by the class.

Only the fat boy, who knows all about being picked on,
picks on the invisible boy, and only when
his classmates untie the ropes of taunts on him
and let him pick someone else to pick on.

Every eye is on the fat boy then, waiting to see his choice.
Some even offer themselves with stinging snickers,
dropping their pants,
but the fat boy's double chin is crueler
and crunchier than the trap set for him;
putting on a black mustache,
he calls out the name of the invisible boy,
the thin one with hemp-colored hair who's not even there
but in a flimsy paper fort of his own;

from a naked tower room
he releases invisible doves that
scour waste baskets for messages,

and now the fat boy,
let loose on his victim,
strangles the doves with his pudgy hands
and throws them back into the invisible boy's
invisible fort.

The class is dismissed,
but the game goes on year after year,
schoolroom after schoolroom,
even without the taunting class,
the fat boy becomes
ever so fat,
the whole class hangs from his belly and jowls,

and the invisible boy of the silent, hemp-colored hair
becomes more invisible inside his invisible fort;

the bricks he scribbles on the paper towers
slowly fade out
like his hemp-colored stare.

{Paul Sohar lives in Warren, New Jersey. Born in Hungary.
Dreamer & Scribbler.}

Dreadful Play

Eternity stood
between the ringing of the bell
and the stepping of my feet
onto the playground.

I was suffocating,
guts swirling
around my stomach pit.

Suddenly the air cracked and nothing mattered
except my fear
and my escape.

I ran—flew—hard as my heart could go
beyond the sea of kids.
Yet she overcame me,
her feet fueled by playground eyes:
a mixture sick with terror and awe.

One quick blow sent my whole body skidding
onto the slick asphalt.
I couldn't get up, couldn't fight back,
couldn't stop my
crybabyface.

The gawking wouldn't stop.

And it is only now
that I know
(it took so long to see)
that it was *her* guilt, *her* shame, and *her* disgrace
plastered painfully on *my* face.

{Carolyn Rice lives in Tiburon, California. Poet & Archaeologist.}

Robert Browning, not the poet

The boy in gym class
who was brown
who got sent home
because his gym shoes
were too worn

showed up one harsh spring day
on my front door step.
His hands were bare.
He'd used his mittens to keep
a waffle warm for me.

We walked to school through the wet.

I thought he was another
pool-eyed deer like me
who stood in fear
numb-tongued and
thirsty
by the water fountain
and waited waited
'til there was safety.

But he was born outside.
Only the wind could bully him.
He knew the rain spoke
the thousand thousand wonders
of all who didn't speak.
He believed the meek
rode horses into heaven.

{Jane Ann Flint lives in Oakland, California. Born and raised in Sioux Falls, South Dakota. Storyteller & Maker.}

Identity

Decades after a man leaves the Church,
still he is called the priest.

Many years since she set down her bow,
a woman remains the cellist.

The one who seduced so many is content
now to sip her tea,
and still she is looked at with envy and hatred.

The one who held life and death
in his mouth
no longer speaks at all, yet still he is feared.

The unmoving dancer rehearses her steps.
Again, perfection eludes her.

Fate loosens its grip. The bruises stay.

{Jane Hirshfield lives in San Francisco Bay Area, California. Grew up in New York City. Poet & Essayist. barclayagency.com/hirshfield.html}

Not Me

I must have been five that summer, because I was a Sandpiper, the youngest group of kids at Waredaka day camp. So my brother would have been nine.

We were waiting for the bus going home. At first it was just my brother and me. But suddenly we were surrounded by a bunch of big and pimply boys. They circled and jeered. Way up close to my brother. Freak! Sissy! You're a kike. Aren't you? Aren't you? You're a kraut and a kike.

They turned to me. That your brother? Your brother's stupid, isn't he? Isn't he. I shook my head yes. Your brother's a freak, isn't he. See, even your sister thinks you're stupid. Your sister says you're a freak.

I chose their side so nothing bad would happen. But I wasn't on the side I belonged. When it began to rain, the big boys left, my brother shaking, and everything got quiet.

{Rose Black lives in Oakland, California. Born and raised in Washington, DC. Poet & Activist. renaissance.com}

They bussed us to the induction center. Inside, I spilled a hundred cups of urine and passed out cigars. When they asked, I was deaf, blind. I was nineteen, and I didn't know what else to do. They gave me an intelligence test, and I answered every question wrong. An officer said, we'll give you another test, and each time they did, my intelligence failed. I was alone in a room with two men. They stood beside me with their guns drawn, and gave me one test after another for hours. One of them said, you son-of-a-bitch, the men you came with are waiting for you outside, and we'll keep them there all night if we have to. He didn't understand, I'd have kept them there forever if I could.

Jupiter, Venus, and Mars are in conjunction beside a crescent moon. Across the road, three young men throw saw blades and knives against a tree. The men shake with a terrible eagerness. Their shrieks are sexual; they could have abandoned themselves to anything, but they've chosen this. That would have killed him, one of them screams. That would have fucking killed him. It echoes off the other side of the canyon, so we must listen to it more than once.

{Gary Young lives in Santa Cruz, California. Born and raised in Santa Ana, California. Poet & Artist. gary-young.net}

A Bet Between Bullies

After the massacre of innocents
Job who lived by *The Book*
        sat shiva for his family
collateral damage by bullies playing
        Mine Is Bigger Than Yours
same revelers who toyed with
        Hector & Odysseus

I'm ranting about YOU up there
        in special seating
did the Job gig play well in your
        V-I-P lounge
did you even notice Hecuba's
        agony as Achilles defiled her
        son in blood-soaked mud
how did our 20th century play
        up there when down here
it went bonkers with all that
        god power in play
tell us what bullies have in store
        for our 21st

since we're not on speaking terms
        no need to respond
just don't expect songs of praise
for those who leave their empathies
        in other galaxies
while waiting for us to self-destruct

time is long overdue for psalms of
        praise to flow in reverse
after all
where would bullies be without
some of us to praise them?

Excerpt from a Letter: Poetry about bullying?

At first I chuckled & ignored the call until I stumbled on a poem (never submitted) molding in my files. Your submission call made me realize how deeply engrained the bully-strain is in the human psyche. Imagine The Bible extolling two power-players betting on who's bigger. They torment an innocent man by killing his spouse and children then charge the victim with the "sin of pride." I mean, talk about bullying! Think of all the preachers today who still miss the point and the rest of us who think we knew the Job story and missed the obvious. Hence the foregoing poem.

{Alan Cohen lives in San Francisco Bay Area and Italy. Born and raised in Boston, Massachusetts. Behavioral Scientist & Poet.}

Burning the Dolls

In 1851, in John Humphrey Noyes' free-love settlement in Oneida, New York, the communally-raised children, encouraged by the adults, voted to burn their dolls as representative of the traditional role of motherhood.

That last night, unable to sleep,
   I prayed with my doll
      under the twisted-star
quilt, then held her close,

her flannel gown warming my cheek,
   her hair made of yarn
      brushing the tears away.
I sang her favorite lullaby,

then she sang it back to me.
   When the sky flared into dawn
      I carried her in my arm—
not crying now for anyone to see—

to my sisters barefoot on the lawn,
   circling the stacked wood, each
      bearing some small body
that stared into the remote sun.

And when the burning was done,
  when her white, Sunday dress
    was transformed to ash
and each perfect, grasping

finger melted upon the coals,
  when her varnished face burst
    in the furnace of my soul,
the waxy lips forever lost,

then I knew I'd no longer pray,
  even with fire haunting me,
    because I hadn't resembled
closely enough my mother,

hadn't withheld my burgeoning
  desire, so like a doll
    concealing what I'd learned
I burned and burned and burned.

The Conversion of Saint Paul

In 1956 I was the shepherd boy
with nothing to offer the infant Jesus.

Kissed goodbye, I left the walk-up
in a white, ankle-length, terrycloth robe,

flailing my grandfather's wooden cane
wrapped from crook to tip in foil.

Secretaries stared from passing buses
at this Biblical apparition

leading his invisible sheep to school,
O little, wild-eyed prophet of Brooklyn!

Older, I portrayed the leper
gifted with half of St. Martin's cloak

and, with paper arrows and red Play-Doh,
evoked the passion of St. Sebastian.

Then I had to fake a terrible fall
to honor the conversion of St. Paul—

when I changed into costume
in the boys' musty coatroom,

Sister Euphrasia knelt to hike
the elastic waistband of my briefs

to better arrange my torn-sheet toga.
In second grade, this ageless ogre

had pasted Easter seals on my skull
and locked me in a cobwebbed cubicle,

pretending to air-mail me to China
where I'd never again see my mother!

Funny enough today, I guess,
but then I pleaded for forgiveness.

Now her sour breath flushed my face
when—classmates clamoring their impatience—

she whispered Jesus
would be judging my performance,

then thrust me from her failing sight
to be apprehended by all that light.

{Michael Waters lives in Ocean, New Jersey. Born and raised in
Brooklyn, New York. Poet & Bon Vivant.}

Yellow Jacket

I hung my olive-green, just-bought
sports coat on a fire plug.
I did nothing. They fought
each other, really.
        – Derek Walcott, "Blues"

"Would you make the whole world a temple?
Be like the sun, and what is within you will warm the Earth."
        – Master Po, Shaolin priest, TV's *Kung Fu*, 1973,
            after Cane witnesses a fight in the market place.

On that third parent, 70s TV, it would have required lens flare: a super-imposition of false anamorphic disks of light, imperfect imitations of the actual sun, fractionated, splaying out on a diagonal to the deliberate padding of a man's simple shoes over searing dunes at dusk. The family's gaudy coffee-table bible would have called for glossy color plates. Christ emerging from the Judean Desert. *Life Magazine*, also on his household's coffee table, would have laid it out folio-sized, in grainy contrasts of black and white. Truth gathers against the sweltering Mississippi sirocco.

But between *Life* and real-life adolescent minds wander in veils of imagination. In the world real to him, Evdokim's world, it started, as always, another hot San Joaquin Valley California afternoon, about 90 degrees, on the other side of the Tierra Arrasada Junior High fence, waiting for the bus.

It was not quite summer. Michael, too lanky for a genuine bully, clowned. A sloppy line had formed but the bus was late and all the other lines of students were gone. It was so hot that any adult supervisors had long since headed for shade in the distance or back to their classroom or office. Michael went up and down the line, halting here and there, to take on a most unlikely pose. Clutching his right ankle in his right hand in the air, like some awkward ballerina warming up, Michael would say "I'm gonna kick your butt." He would then motion an off balance kick, more of a gesture, toward a kid's face with his foot. Alternating, both feet on the ground at times, he puffed out his chest and got into the face of each tired, guileless unsuspecting, randomly—no—specially selected, docile innocent. But Evdokim saw Michael's act coming and knew, as the heat pounded down where they stood there in the rutted dirt like passengers on the once muddied banks of a now dried-up river waiting to embark on a non-existent adventure, just what he would do.

Michael came up to Evdokim with his stocky henchman, Roland Parson, tagging along in his cowboy boots, laughing. When Michael got close Evdokim was ready. He'd had enough: enough of the merciless heat sizzling across playground pavement, enough of a day of classrooms without air-conditioning, enough of the waiting, enough trouble at home, enough of Michael's fooling. As his foot flapped toward Evdokim's face, as his tongue followed flapping the same spiel: "I'm gonna kick your bu..." Evdokim's hand flashed outward succeeded by a simple open-handed tap with follow-through, up, up, up, just below Michael's Achilles' heel. Michael went down hard on the hardpan-like clay and dirt, and for a moment, Evdokim was sorry. He thought Michael had broken his tailbone in his fall. Yet only laughter from the crowd broke—including Roland's. Still, Evdokim had only hurt Michael, made him mad. He got up rubbing his ass, dusting off. Michael's slight chest swelling again like a blowfish, he came close to Evdokim, almost spitting in his face.

"You're gonna die! I'm 'onna kill you!" He didn't though, because just then their mad bus driver, who took joy in hitting every curve or turn at top speed, had rounded the bend in that yellow-jacketed sports car they called a school bus.

A kind of cheer went out. Everyone shuffled in that moment to put the line into some kind of order. And the impending promise of a fight, so welcome in the heat and the boredom of waiting, was all but forgotten.

"You gonna die. You gonna die!" Michael screeched like a parrot. However, the bus doors had opened and the last line of remaining students were filing in. Almost forgetting, Michael and Roland scrambled forcing their way somewhere into the line a bit behind Evdokim. As the seating commenced all of the closed windows clicked open, their clasps skating over the notches like firecrackers going off, and a warm breeze, which gave the illusion of being cool, whipped into the faces of the children as the bus departed. Still, a number of loud threats continued from where Michael sat on the bus ride home, so that when they had finally reached their stop—a parking lot at Alpha Beta Market—and stepped out onto the large paved parking lot, Michael came at Evdokim again, blustering, and threatening.

The bus driver, who couldn't help but hear Michael's threats along the ride, came down off his seat, down the stairs of the bus, and made a few official sounding threats of his own to Michael, so the whole thing looked over, until the bus rolled away. Then, once again, Michael puffed at Evdokim. Yet the more Michael blustered, the more Evdokim knew Michael was afraid. The Rose Avenue crowd was egging Michael on, and the John Sutter crowd pushing Evdokim forward, probably led by Mike Gastelem, a big guy Evdokim had gone to grammar school with, always looking for trouble, and no real friend of his.

Yet finally, though it wasn't easy for Evdokim, he turned. Just walked away. Left Michael there bellowing and posturing to no one in particular. Evdokim made his way through the crowd. Then he crossed Orangeburg Avenue with a few others, his thoughts on TV's Kwai Chang Caine, on Jesus Christ, on Martin Luther King, Jr., and on Caesar Chavez.

Along Allen Street on the way home, he fielded questions from mini-skirted Nichole Vuckovich, pretty as ever—who hadn't spoken to Evdokim since the sixth grade.

"Why didn't you fight him? Are you afraid?"

"No. It was his move," Evdokim managed to say as if it were a chess game. Still he was thinking but never got out, he had, after all, knocked Michael on his ass.

Evdokim never saw Michael on morning bus rides to school. But he had expected some possible confrontation with Michael the next day on the bus ride home. It didn't come though. On the bus, Evdokim saw Michael at the further end gazing out the window, oddly quiet, almost sullen. Tom Shields, an elementary school friend, told him, "Yesterday, after you walked away, Gastelem beat him up *for* you."

The bus lurched forward, its seat-beltless contents rocked as it went on in its rough way. Evdokim understood then that right thinking and right actions were only in one's head. He perceived that the world too goes on in its callous, corrupting way. So much so that it's tough, even, for one individual padding upon its surface, to make a point. Maybe not so surprisingly the *third parent*—second for Evdokim not counting a couple of older brothers—had let him down. But it really stung to think that Master Po was only half right. Sure, the world could never be a temple—let alone he a priest. But—though he didn't know about China—he knew it would be damned arrogant of anyone to think that being like the sun in the heat of the unforgiving San Joaquin Valley would ever be of any use at all.

{Vincent Joseph Noto lives in Portland, Oregon. Born and raised in Modesto, California. Writer & Poet. https://sites.google.com/site/noto}

The Tyrants and the Gone Daughter

They followed sleep and hissed inside her head
Brutal ghosts who wouldn't fade into the night
They circled her like beasts around the moon
To rip out her light and leave it for dead

She felt naked clothed with many layers
And motherless though that falcon peered
Out the window to watch her walk from school
Twisting crystal beads and whispering prayers:

Please lord above bring those bullies bright love
Fill their blood with meadows and birds
Make them not too proud to cry their pain aloud
As I cradle mine, depleted mourning dove

She lived fastened to the wall, a blanched, wilting rose
There was no shelter from those infectors
Quick black beaks shot song-less from their eyes,
Devoured her last millet of joy

In the end it was she who flew. Only her body,
Only her life. The bullies, jewel-fingered, gold
Crosses of murdered love tangled in the
Sweat of their chests, faced frozen walls, each

Alone, each nailed, each waiting on the precipice
Carved just for them, hungering for they knew
Not what in a world devoid of illumination
And love—the beginning of non-existence

{Katherine Hastings lives in Santa Rosa, California. Poet & Poet Laureate
of Sonoma County. wordtemple.com}

Evacuation Day, June 5, 1942

At an empty station, beside
the train tracks' quiet gleam,
it's dusk, the in-between time
of a warm June evening.
With brakes screeching, a truck
skids to a stop at the platform,
spilling out young soldiers,
rifles slung over their backs,
drunkenly shoving each other,
shattering a windowpane in the station.

With a hiss, a black train creeps in.
Silent, the Japanese families approach,
dressed in their Sunday best.
Numbered and tagged,
they line up to board, heavy
with what they are allowed to carry.

Throughout the night, the train carries
its freight from their Yakima Valley homes
to an unknown future. Soldiers order
shades drawn, parade the aisles, point rifles,
as though their weary prisoners could escape.

Pulling into the stockyard,
the train's shriek signals arrival.
But still in darkness, the cargo
hears only the clang of the closing gates.

{Jodi L. Hottel is a poet and teacher.}

Intent on Restoring Disorder

history lumbers on
unstoppable
insinuating
while birds and everyone else
sing the same phrases
over and over

fleeing angels correct their course
seeking a fresh exit strategy
as the dung beetle orients itself
by the light of the milky way
its life as flat as a comic strip

the clouds whisper to each other
left only to bear witness
they sigh the name
of the space in between

although details are in dispute
time goes by
in an amnesic drift
the past with exultation and ache
anticipates the future's return

{Les Bernstein lives in Mill Valley, California. Born in New York.
   Poet & Cenosillicaphobic.}

Utopia

A home where there won't be yelling
When you open the front door
It's too loud to hear yourself think
A school where there are no stereotypes
You stand, in a circle staring
Making a life story of someone from what they look like
A town where you can feel you're needed
When all you want to do is run away
Because where you live you don't feel wanted
A city where there is no stealing
You don't have to watch
Your back, while you walk down a street
A place where there are no hurt feelings
When someone crosses the line,
Goes too far
A world where we can be ourselves
I want these lives to become realistic
I need our Earth to become Utopia

{Gigi Wyatt is in 9th Grade at Tamalpais High School, Mill Valley, California.}

Dear Friends and Fellow Graduates of Middle School,

William Shakespeare summed it up with a few simple words: the wheel has come full circle. I'd like to reflect on things not just about me, but also you, Fellow Classmates. Over our class's three years, we have learned much together; we have worked together for so long that we are completely used to each other. Together our moral, social, and political ideals have changed as we completed assignments together, experienced Challenge Day, and went on field trips as a class. We have "branched out," tried new electives; we've been to new places and we've done new things.

It's only now that I take pleasure in my cold, grey, and blustery bike rides to school in the morning that give me a headache and numb hands—then the hot, taxing ordeal of getting my bike back up the hill at the end of the school day. Before, I saw it as just a downside to my day. I have acquired a taste for better literature; I've worked with (and against) my computer to finish pieces of art, writing or video, and I have worked harder and harder to beat the deadlines for assignments and homework. My friends have helped me prioritize, to learn what is important and what is not. All this change is due to you, my classmates, and our teachers, who (if we know it or not) are always striving to help us change.

I know firsthand that the impressions you make on others and how you treat them not only affect you, but also affect them. You could spark a new idea in them, give them the drive to do something better, give them courage—or in contrast you could send their spirits plummeting, crushing them underneath cruel jokes, pranks, denial, and criticism. I admit, I have been less than a model citizen, maybe because others treated me poorly before I came to this school. Yet I have learned that in the end, it's up to me how I treat others, and forgive those who have hurt my feelings before.

Impressions count, but you can't appeal to everyone. Try to keep at least a small group of friends that you know are loyal and will help you out at all times and stay true to the end; for me, it includes two people that still live up north, from where I came. Here are some lessons my friends have taught me through their actions, words and deeds: don't bother yourself with appealing to the "popular" crowd just so that you can feel more accepted; your true friends are those who count. Focus hard on study, and it will pay off in the future—but don't be afraid to have fun. Do something challenging every day after school. Meet the goals you set for yourself. Give your education the respect it deserves.

Education is arguably the most powerful tool humans have ever invented, and I want everyone to know how lucky we are that we belong to such a good district. Education is a singular means to almost any end, and whoever thinks it isn't important at all times is fooling himself. I'd like to thank all of our teachers for helping us to achieve the lofty heights of our graduates: motivated learners, creative problem solvers, engaged citizens, and all that jazz. Nelson Mandela said, "Education is the most powerful weapon which you can use to change the world."

I'm glad that the twisting pathways of life have brought me here today, in a beautiful place with great teachers, an awesome education, and great friends; and given me new hopes, dreams, and goals. I hope you are happy with where you are, as well, and have people to help you on your own personal journeys. We still have a way to go, though, and just a few more rotations of the wheel to complete before we go out into the world. See you on the flip side!

{Dylan Losee is in the 8th grade at Delmar Middle School, Tiburon, California.}

Mixed Doubles

We begged them not to play.
We didn't want to watch them
get beaten by the Hellburns
or Feldsteins or Rosenblooms
as valets crammed the parking lot
with Mercedes. My father
slapped at each ball, lopped
at the volleys, wobbled
on girlish ankles too thin
for his weight. He liked to hiss
at bad calls, curse a good serve,
dig his racket down into the clay.
And when he ordered our mother
around the court, we watched her
run like a squirrel on a nut-chase,
frilly lace on her tennis panties
sticking out from under her skirt
like a muted, cut-off bridal train.

The Girl Who Hanged Herself

And when I think of her legs dangling
in stiff blue jeans, her snapped neck,

and her body limp over the bathtub,
I think of her digging her name

into the school's cheap furniture,
how all I knew of this girl was that scratch,

the fine-lined, heart-shaped tattoo on her breast
that jiggled as she walked in late to my class,

and the way she waved goodbye to her friends
as I stood at the blackboard,

brushing chalk dust off my skirt.

{Cindy Milwe lives in Venice, California. Born in suburban Connecticut
and called to New York City in her teens. Writer & Teacher.}

Thirteen

In the morning
he searched for answers
and found there were no answers.
And as easy as it was to turn a page
in a magazine, the easier it was to think
of his fragile body floating free;
and what about words, his poems,
already forgotten, already a back issue.

In the afternoon
he used his Sunday dress-up tie
to hang himself in the ill-lit hallway
at his junior high.
How did he get in, everyone wanted to know?
There were signs of depression.
There were the gay taunts
at school and in his neighborhood.

In the evening,
in the ocean, everything changes
and begins again.

Laguna, California

One August day
at St. Anne's Beach,
Walker and Beau
dumped out my new purse,
danced in the sand,
singing *Jew Girl, Jew.*

When I cried
and a few people glanced our way,
the boys retrieved my belongings,
each item
lifted from its gritty resting place.

There they stood,
two of the best-looking guys in school,
muscular and tall,
shaggy, bleached hair,
dark glasses hiding blue eyes.

Walker spun around and left,
but Beau raised his hand in apology,
momentarily obscuring
the sun.

{Rafaella Del Bourgo lives in Berkeley, California. Born in Hollywood, California.}

Charlie Howard's Descent

Between the bridge and the river
he falls through
a huge portion of night;
it is not as if falling

is something new. Over and over
he slipped into the gulf
between what he knew and how
he was known. What others wanted

opened like an abyss: the laughing
stock-clerks at the grocery, women
at the luncheonette amused by his gestures.
What could he do, live

with one hand tied
behind his back? So he began to fall
into the star-faced section
of night between the trestle

and the water because he could not meet
a little town's demands,
and his earrings shone and his wrists
were as limp as they were.

I imagine he took the insults in
and made of them a place to live;
we learn to use the names
because they are there,

familiar furniture: *faggot*
was the bed he slept in, hard
and white, but simple somehow,
queer something sharp

but finally useful, a tool,
all the jokes a chair,
stiff-backed to keep the spine straight,
a table, a lamp. And because

he's fallen for twenty-three years,
despite whatever awkwardness
his flailing arms and legs assume
he is beautiful

and like any good diver
has only an edge of fear
he transforms into grace.
Or else he is not afraid,

and in this way climbs back
up the ladder of his fall,
out of the river into the arms
of the three teenage boys

who hurled him from the edge—
really boys now, afraid,
their fathers' cars shivering behind them,
headlights on—and tells them

it's all right, that he knows
they didn't believe him
when he said he couldn't swim,
and blesses his killers

in the way that only the dead
can afford to forgive.

{Mark Doty lives in New York City and on the east end of Long Island.
Born in Maryville, Tennessee. Poet & Memoirist. markdoty.org}

Dear Mr. Joseph,

I wrote this letter. My name is Mike. My first sixteen years I spent in a home for me. I have autism. My brother Chris who I never remember got me out. I miss my teacher Mrs. Reese who is very kind and beautiful but it is better now. Chris could not find me. He's 24 years old now and is married to Susan my new sister. They have no children. She is kind and wants a baby wish I hope for her. She typed this letter but I wrote this letter because when I was sent to a regular school not everyone was nice to me. They said I eat funny. And talk funny. I was sad. But Mr. Principal talk to all of us and said this is bad for me and them too. This book my brother told me about I wish to be in because it is a good thing. Thank you Mr. Poet for reading this I hope you are happy like me too. I wrote this letter and Chris says it is good.

Mike

{Michael C. lives in Michigan. 10th Grade. Wants to be a writer and teacher.}

After the School Picnic

He seems ordinary, blue tee shirt, white lettering. He looks down at his daughter, saying words I can't hear, slaps her face once, twice, a third time. She stands awkwardly in front of him, not crying, waiting, and he points to the bench. She walks over, sits carefully, legs almost reaching the concrete. He leans against a car, trying to appear at ease, the dark green of the driver's door almost matching the rest of it. Minutes go by. He motions for the girl to come back to him, puts his hands on her shoulders, perhaps saying something comforting, as her hands search each other for a home.

{Stephanie Mendel lives in Belvedere, California. Born and raised in Pittsburgh, Pennsylvania. Senior & Poet. stephaniemendel.com}

Cross Dressing Trucker in West Texas

I automatically
dial the Merkel Police

when he pulls
in because

he gets
a beating

every time

he sports
those black nylons

and stiletto
heels

in the
Flying J
Truck Stop

Shower Room

{Sheryl L. Nelms lives in Clyde, Texas. Born in Marysville, Kansas, raised in Nebraska & Kansas. Poet & Painter.}

If swear words trouble you, I suggest you read no further

An except from "With Fire, from Abroad: Memories with ADD"

Fear, have you felt it before? Really felt it? That giant, invisible snake squeezing you, slowing your motions as it tightens your muscles? What about Despair? Despair as you see your whole past, present and future poisoned by not fitting in, condemned to medications and repeated failures caused by Self-Doubt. What about Terror, perhaps my least favorite flavor, mixed with Dread. Imagine being surrounded by a group of boys who want to play with you (no not with you like in football, play with you as a cat plays with a mouse.). They want to watch you suffer because apparently you have "great reactions." For their enjoyment. Sick fucks. All I wanted was to be left alone, escape this universe, crawl up in a bed and go to sleep, and in sleep find a doorway to another world, a reality that didn't have to end, where the monsters disappeared and nice people lived and loved each other and things actually made sense and worked out and people didn't violate me. A place I could escape to, forever. Someplace safe.

And to my classmates, to the folks that hit me, some with fists, others with words, and to the girls who whipped my heart with their words, to you whose eyes avoided mine, to you who never responded when I opened a most tender heart to reveal a long hidden and despairing desire, fuck you to hell. I have to smile. I have love for you too. Fuck you, fuck you, fuck you for hurting me. Yet, our solid hearts must be broken so that a wider river of love can course through our veins. So fuck you for hurting me, and for hurting me, I thank you.

[Charles A. Wright lives as a global nomad. Born in Berkeley, and raised in Piedmont, and Lake Tahoe, California.]

August 4, 1994

Dear Jacob:

Since I was your age, I put up with people like you who made me the target of their hatred toward gays. After making "rude comments," they said they were "only joking." And, like you, they figured I would "laugh and walk away," because they assumed gay men were wimps who would not fight back.

Indeed, I would not fight back because I did not want my coworkers and clients to know I am gay. So I kept quiet. My silence not only encouraged you to believe it was okay to harass gays, but that I enjoyed it.

But after a long string of your gay "jokes" in which you said I slept with dogs (one of the worst insults I suffered as a teen), I could no longer laugh and walk away. For the first time in my life, I stood up to someone who verbally abused me and told him to stop. Unfortunately, you were on the receiving end of years of pent-up rage, but you were the one joyfully pressing all of the wrong buttons.

Please understand, Jacob, I do not hate you. In fact, I find you to be a very likeable person who has a lot of potential. And I believe you do not hate me either, but letting you continue to belittle and berate me would not be love, either. And if it means anything to you, I forgive you.

And, yes, you can send me the mug you made in ceramics. I would be glad to have it.

Sincerely,
André Le Mont Wilson

{André Le Mont Wilson lives in Hercules, California. Born and raised in Los Angeles, California. Storyteller & Poet.}

MATTHEW LIPPMAN

Dear James:

I don't know why I remember rugs, I do, probably because I love time on the floor, down there, next to the smell of things, the lint, where the dog peed, where the pineapple went. You had this fireplace in your house and we stuck Matchbox Cars in there even though you were a fat, single kid with no dad. I used to come over to your house when my family moved to New Rochelle. You were my first friend, really, even though in the rolling history of my life I always say it was the Bloom/ Kennedy kids. The truth is, it was you, and you might have been gay, even before I knew what gay was, but nobody liked you. I liked you but maybe I just liked that you took me out of my loneliness, my 11-year-old loneliness, and then when something better came along, I dropped you like a cat cut from the strings of its parachute. Or maybe I just liked your orange rug because it was orange but I remember most that I did a bad thing. Bad as in throwing you off of me like a 1976 shawl, all flowery and wool, to go listen to Bad Company and Born To Run with my cooler friends who weren't cool at all. Don't you hate that, the word cool, the way it ruins whole generations of young people because they don't wear the right shoes, suck the right dick, hang out in the right clubs? I have wanted to apologize to you for almost 40 years and haven't figured out how; even this letter doesn't figure out how to tell me, or any of us, how to be good people. Maybe you are born that way—all goodness and juice. I think you were born that way and why you let me roll around with you on your floor and throw Matchbox Cars up into the air. We watched them like satellites, in awe, our hands touching, as they came crashing down to earth and there we were, hysterical and tender the way it should have stayed, even though it's presumptuous of me to think I broke your heart when all along it's my heart that's been broken and why this letter helps me believe that I can put it back together.

Thank you.

My deepest love, Matthew

{Matthew Lippman lives in Boston, Massachusetts. Born and raised in New York City. Poet & Teacher. matthewlippmanpoetry.com}

Twenty-One

Look at him. He's six feet four
lost between worlds of structure
and imagination. A future shaped
like a question mark...curiosity
beaten out of him in second grade
when his mocha-colored hand waved
to be called on made him different,
moved to the back of the room
for juxtaposing letters on the page.
Not one teacher caught his frustration
of seeing words...differently.

He hits the target, like baseballs
thrown to him, a home-run kid.
He tells me he loves history,
the video games he plays
to relieve his stress, the mystery
of identity. He's somewhere in a line
between college and unemployment.
"Who's the black guy?" they ask.
He's half and half. Coffee and cream.
He seems...different.

He was a curiosity when he moved to a place
where confederate flags waved from
antennae of junk cars, a cross burned
on a lawn. He practiced high school football,
couldn't take a shower in the locker room.
"We don't allow any slaves in here," they said
and blocked his way. He quit. The school bus
was dangerous. "Anyone for white power?"
a kid shouted. Half the bus stood up
and raised clenched fists.

We learn to sort by color, shape and size.
How to put things in boxes. The odd
ones that do not match are set aside.
The unmatched ones can see things
differently. I ask, "Are you afraid?"
He says, "Who's gonna mess with me?
They see a six foot four inch black guy."
I caution him, "Don't wear a hoodie.
No saggy pants. No hands in pockets."
He moves now...differently.

———⟫◆⟪———

"Twenty-One," is a poem about my 21-year-old grandson. He is racially mixed; I never thought this would be a problem in California. He was raised by my daughter (who was a single mother when she gave birth to him at 17). He was the most out-going, charming, bright kid until he hit 2nd grade and discovered he was different. He was taken out of the regular high school in northern California, graduating from a special school because he was being bullied so badly that it became dangerous. He is now afraid to be in crowds and is struggling to get back into junior college.

{Barbara Welch Brooks lives in Novato, California.
Raised in Philadelphia, Pennsylvania. Poet & Dream-catcher.}

White and Black, Black and White

– Que saudadel

I love Brazil yes love its fragrance its markets its street
Sounds its saints my people my poverty my pickpockets

I hate Brazil where I'm white not black where blacks
Love being white because of one drop of Portuguese blood

I hate Brazil where blacks with every drop of black blood
Bleed and bleed red blood where white blacks bleed

Red blood red crosses red sunsets red brick red sands
Their beautiful children their beautiful wives their Brazil

I love Brazil love my white black black white children
My white black black white mulher my Brazil my jungle

I love America my City of Brotherly Love its Liberty Bell
Its El trains its Dutch hidden river its Eagles and Phillies

I hate America where I'm black not white where whites
Love being white and blacks love being black I hate

Crime and rats and black men beating black men white
Men stopping turning from black men walking this way that way

I love and I hate I hate and I love white and black and white
I will be whatever you want me to be Brazil America

America I want to love you and you love me Brazil
I don't want to be black and white and white and black

I will not

{Matheus Carvalho lives in Philadelphia, Pennsylvania. Born and raised in Porto Alegre, Rio Grande do Sul, Brazil. Painter & Poet-Taxi Driver.}

Nineteen Forty

Black Beast, 1940, a stabile by Alexander Calder

pinning its four wings into earth
    like daggers bent on catharsis
a black creature   unassailable nightmare
    suddenly in the light
        in its bolted black skin

it stabs the sky with its other
    horse-sized wings
four arching points raised in silence
    as if to make sure the earth can hear itself
        being punctured

the Big War they called it   fifty million dead
    a monster that spewed its foul presence
across continents   even The Great Alexander
    packaged shock and awe
        like liberation

a black beast   hope slips its moorings
    the world on tenterhooks
furnaces and mass graves and the usual ethnic cleansing
    the black beast inside every man
        twitching   flicking its tail

{William Landis lives in Auburn, California. Poet & Artist.
willlandis.blogspot.com}

The Bottle Tree

I was so proud, Mama, to get that robe, to help
plant a cross with our county's finest men.
They let me have two swigs of shine and load up
Papa's shotgun.

That boy knelt on a hard-swept floor
below a char-drawn likeness of Jesus.
In a rightful fury, his ma'am fought like three
big men; her sorrow bit like bile
into the roof of my mouth.

We dragged him to their bottle tree, and Mama,
those bottles made a sucking sound and poured out
colored moonlight at our feet. We staggered about
grinning like fear

as someone shot the barking dog; we laughed when another
tore down the damp unmentionables that snapped
on a single taut line.

As the rope was drawn around a limb, too near
a hollowed gourd with purple martin eggs,
I raised my hood to throw up supper on my boots,
then helped to paint a home with kerosene and fire.

Since then my children raised up children who play
with brown-skinned ones; and those who'd force it otherwise
are mostly hair and bones.

But the lowest branches caught the flames that night;
today the wounds still seep, and the heat-shocked
bottles dance and howl—maybe for reckoning.

Here, even animals stay wary: the deer won't rut,
dogs won't lift to pee, and till I too go on to Hell,
the martins won't come again.

Because I'm a pig

To make Him forget
if for only a moment
the smell of cooking flesh
I danced about
the penultimate moment
in maddening spins—learned
by shaking shit from cloven hooves.
Oh yes

I am practiced
in pirouettes.
I'd the wit to postpone the holocaust.
But for what purpose?
you'll ask
with the rest of my ilk
incredulous on the truck,
and the truck always comes
empty in the spring.

Warm in my shrinking
corner of unsoiled straw
I grow fatter still
on my disgrace.
The thaw will find me
too corn-fed-tremendous
to dance—a craven pet.

But I've a carnivore's conceit
and one should never forget
the hog's taste for meat;
yet the Farmer
passes closer every day,
like a conditional friend,
whistling
and impudently alone.

{Allen M Weber lives in Hampton, Virginia. Born and raised in Bangor, Michigan. Teacher & Student.}

My Last Breath

my last breath will not put me to sleep
but will wake me up in a spa with a Japanese soak tub
where I slip into water still as glass and
sink down into startling heat
all the striving will dissolve
and I will see how beautiful and foolish I was
how weak and scared and precious
all the things that tripped me up held grace
that will now seep in to me
my list of complaints and questions will blur in the gauzy steam
then evaporate, leaving me wise, buoyant, perfect
except for one thing, I want everybody in on it
so I pull myself out of the tub, wrap in a fat white towel
go dripping back to the old country to poke around, look for trouble
there are lots of us there, beefy Linnea the grade school bully
works beside Bin Laden tapping on shoulders, whispering in ears
"take a breath, find common ground"
experts, they get the toughest cases

{Judith Goedeke lives in Laurel, Maryland. Born and raised in Baltimore, Maryland. Seeker.}

Perfect Target

—how they'd leer when he walked up
to them with his face flower-open, then
one would shrug a book-ballasted backpack
to sprawl him out flat on the asphalt.

How they'd tell him that the teacher
wanted, no really wanted him to jump
on the lunch table to see if it would break,
the apology note after note after note

he dutifully wrote. How at bath time
he'd say the bruises and scrapes were
nothing, nothing, leave it alone,
Mom, don't make it worse Mom.

How one time they cornered him
behind the storage shed and stoned him
in a hail of green oranges, left him
facedown bloodsnotted in dirt.

How he braided in three strands the lanyard
of his middle school years;
the hours and hours spent pacing
the playground alone,

the play dates and parties
he was never invited to, the chairs
pulled away
just before he sat down.

{Rebecca Foust lives in Kentfield, California. Born and raised in Altoona,
Pennsylvania. Mother & Writer.}

Those Boys Who Were Fourteen

in the locker room after Tiger basketball practice
saw the fight, heard who started it, knew who threw

first punch, but it was our son in the ER getting
his head stitched up on Saturday night

and when I went to his coach, hat in hand,
begging another chance, he told me

all about *the rules,* how both boys were off
the team, but he'd go to the others, who had

years ahead of them to grow into their feet
get rid of their teeth's braces. If a single pimply

face would say it was not the fault of our son,
he'd let him back on the team. *I don't hold out*

much hope, he said handing me his hanky,
they're only fourteen. Never offer your tears

to a man without hope, he knows his characters,
spiders they like to kill, the ones who'll laugh

when a wing's pulled off a butterfly. My son came
to supper, couldn't eat, left his jersey, sneakers,

jock strap on his dresser like a shrine. The sutures
were lifted, left a small scar, but silver Number 10

flashed its hill's broken mirror for months
when I made his bed. When the coach called, his

voice cracked asking the uniform be returned.
The other boy? Had baseball, football, the lead

in the freshman play. Never rinse off your hoe
before the garden's done. There's still time

I believe somebody wants to come clean.
Wherever you are, call me collect,
                    I'll come, your house or mine.

Milkweed

When I tell my husband we need to plant it
he tells me *Honey, it's just a weed* and *where*

would we sow it? Already, most of the bees
are gone, the queens race around hives

like their hair's on fire. Forests are auctioned
off like slaves, and when I tell him the Monarch

butterflies are dwindling, milkweed's the only
place they lay their eggs, he sits down to read.

All around us, chemicals burst seams of gas,
aneurysms blow, wells hemorrhage.

Another loaded gun's pressed to Blair mountain's
soft temple in southern West Virginia.

In Nigeria, men with machetes/grenades, an all
girls' school, children taken alive to kneel in hell.

Wisdom, mercy, love.
There must be seed,
        but where's the ground to grow it?

{Jeanne Bryner lives in Newton Falls, Ohio since age four when her
parents moved from Appalachia to find work. Artist & Healer.}

Passages

My brother guffawed as *Lord
of the Flies* fell from my bag
alongside the rest of my life:

a confetti of drawings and papers,
candy wrappers and worn erasers.
I cringed. Already that fall

he had mauled *Great Expectations*
and *The Good Earth*. Dotted with holes,
the books looked like bait

used on shark hunts. I had lied
at school, maintained I lost
what my brother claimed

as tribute, again and again
punching my covers
with a rusted steak knife.

After each strike, he'd open up
the volume to see how far
he had penetrated. A snort

of recognition escaped
as he snatched his latest victim.
Then he dropped the novel

and turned with a sigh—
the closest we ever came to
an understanding.

{Noel Sloboda lives in York, Pennsylvania. Writer & Dog Trainer.
www2.yk.psu.edu/sites/njs16/}

Cross Country

This was a game of dares: get the girl who won't
undress or shower after a run.

But when they held her down, peeled off her
shorts, her white panties, she didn't struggle.

Nor as they tore off her t-shirt and her sports
bra yet not her shoes, ankle-tape, or socks.

Mute, eyes closed, the girl lay there as they mocked
her unshaved armpits, the sparse pubic curls,

the outie where an innie should have been.
They were hooting like hyenas. *Pack mentality,*

the girl told herself. Then, without moving from
the locker room floor, she began to stretch,

and then she began to run, run across a long,
swathe of meadow to a steep trail, run as if

her life depended on it, run with the freedom
of an unclothed body. She was running pursued

by a swarm of bees, a murder of crows, a herd of
asses, and she ran and kept on running from

danger, running, running, outrunning
her pursuers, running, running, until the last

Jenny in the herd turned off the light
and closed the locker room door behind her

Like It Was

I want to be part of your program, he said.
There is no program.

I don't like it here. I want it like it was.
We all want it like it was.

Then where's the map?
There is no map.

But, listen, I love you.
And I love you.

Doesn't seem like it. Then why am I here?
You attacked me. You hurt me.

But I want to be on your program, he said.
There is no more program....

{Susan Terris lives in San Francisco, California. Born & raised in St. Louis, Missouri. Writer & Risk-taker. susanterris.com}

Cul-de-sac

"There is now, in my mouth, this sharp chain. And it never
comes out" – Dysart (*Equus*, Peter Shaffer)

Last afternoon, I saw a teenage boy
naked in the wooded valley beside our house.
My son, on my left hip, making horsy sounds.
The boy's upright back shone among pines.
He was kneeling on a couverture of needles
buckled with early crocuses. I kissed my son's temple,
kept walking, but his soft woof
made me look again. The boy's buttocks,
taut—a dancer's in mid-fouetté—
and before him, barely visible
next to the neighbor's weathered tool shed,
a dog. The dog still—stilled—and I turned my back
to the quiet woods, stumbled across scruffy lawn,
waited behind the bedroom window.
They emerged from the valley, boy and dog,
the hooded kid who dribbles the ball cul-de-sac
to cul-de-sac late afternoons, mute lab
always at his side—and I thought of Brindi,
the mutt raped for weeks by two of my street children.
They'd stormed into the office, placed the bundle
on my desk: blood soaking the sweatshirts
in which they'd wrapped her. She didn't lift her head.
The boys' bare chests all scabs and scratches—no goosebumps,
though snow winds barbed our windows.
This is the only favor we'll ever ask, we swear.
They kissed her neck and ears, turned around,
then added from the threshold:
When she heals we want her back.
Behind the window, my son hammered my hip.

To Ovidiu, Whose Voice I Still Don't Remember

Once I broke a window and for three months
had to share the first-row desk with you, Ovidiu,
Gypsy boy whose companionship
teachers used as punishment.
I had forgotten you and your eight years
less than a rod away from the teacher's desk
till that 3:00 a.m. when the crowning baby
was no baby at all but the sharp push
of a new terror: when did I blot out
the memory of being cruel,
                    for I must have...
Did I make sure my leg never brushed against
yours, did I dodge your look by convincing
myself the ink stains on my palm required
full attention, did I believe the coarse
charges or wonder, at least once, about your mother,
a nurse, admonished publicly at the biweekly meetings?
I'd have had to care enough to make even indifference
matter, make it send forth its ghost. But there is
no ghost twenty years later, and I *could* say this:
we all suffered. At ten we each had at least one
alcoholic parent (your father the only one mentioned),
at twelve we used few words to seal friendship,
fearing each other—anyone could be the informer
—even this baby waiting to turn in the birth canal.

{Mihaela Moscaliuc lives in Ocean, New Jersey. Born and raised in
 Romania. Poet-Translator & Chocoholic.}

Disassemble

You took a bicycle
by the handlebars
and twisted it
into the head of a bull.

Pablo Picasso, you
had many muses.
Their names were
Olga, Ferdinande, Dora,
Marie-Therese and Jacqueline.

With Olga you danced
and danced, but
Olga's conventional stage
was much too small. You
whirled away with Ferdinande.

The other muses you lit into,
tore apart and put together
until one began to resemble
the next and then each
disappeared altogether.

Some, like Humpty Dumpty,
could not put themselves
back together again.
Two came completely undone,
one by the rope, another by the gun.

Now, Pablo Picasso, I
make you my muse,
I disassemble you
according to my will.
I dance away. Whole.

{Linda Enders lives in Terra Linda, California. Born in Oregon's
Willamette Valley. Nature Lover & Musician.}

Lunch Song

His name was Joel.
I never spoke to him.
Everyone knew everyone else
in junior high. Names
and odd behaviors
and who could be a friend.

He was tall, quiet, blond.
Pencils in his pocket, probably a math whiz.
He sat with a boy in big glasses
on the bus and on the bench at lunch.

But once, he gave us riffs
on an uneaten sandwich.
Tapping syncopated rhythms with his pencil
on a plastic thermos, he sang out:

There was a turkey
His name was Ham
Ham-ham-hammie turkey
Born from a chicken queer

He felt into the beat, stretched out.
We crowded in to hear his talk-song,
a lit fuse. The ragged edge of his voice
still hot as it touched our ears.

I listened for him on the bus home,
but a dull hum bustled down the aisle
as if he'd never sung. Someone,
someone sank back again.

{Janet Jennings lives in San Anselmo, California. Born and raised in
Illinois and California. Poet & Mother.}

A Bully in Fourth Grade

In the schoolyard right at the end of recess, I saw my friend stuff a dirty tissue from the muddy ground into little Hannah's mouth. Hannah had a pageboy haircut that Leslie had decided to hate.

And don't you dare tell on me
she threatened in a low voice to her victim,
as Hannah began to cry,
    just say that you fell.
then Leslie walked triumphantly into the classroom with the rest of us.

At our desks, Mr. Roebuck asked Hannah why she was crying. He seemed impatient with the class—some kids being rambunctious and one with a secret drama. A pitcher in the minor leagues before he married, Mr. Roebuck was known to peg a blackboard eraser at an inattentive student's head, all the way from his desk at the front of the room. Sometimes he missed, whacking a complete innocent.

Once he struck Hannah's friend, Mindy, by mistake. She was a tiny girl, new that year, who always looked about to faint—who looked as if she needed more food. Mindy's thin brown hair remained dusted with white chalk that day, like she had suddenly grown old. Mr. Roebuck apologized, but by then I knew he was not to be trusted; our teacher's aim was reckless.

    Why are you crying, Hannah?
Mr. Roebuck inquired again, obviously agitated for the moment at being a teacher, and not a famous baseball player, because little girls were emotional sometimes, kept their heads bowed, and gave no clear signals on how he was meant to manage them.

    Does anyone know why Hannah is crying?
This time our teacher's voice boomed out to the entire class, now grown quiet, but no one knew (except my friend) and me, who remained stuck in my seat in mute misery, overwhelmed by my inability to voice the truth I wanted to reveal—that my whole heart and body begged to stand up and shout:

Leslie stuffed a dirty tissue in Hannah's mouth just to be mean
and told her not to tell!

Then Hannah looked up, not out of courage, but out of fear, her pale, round face streaked by tears.
   I tripped and fell,
she managed to mumble, before her eyes went down again to her desk as if its blank surface could offer some kind of solace, some kind of friend... and now the memory ends.

⋙◈⋘

I left Vermont a long time ago, but my brother still lives there. He's in the habit of reading the obituaries. Recently, he sent me a clipping—all the way to San Francisco. It was about Hannah, dead from cancer.
   Wasn't she in your class in elementary school?
He scrawled in pen at the top of the flimsy newsprint.

   Yes,
I answered to myself, Hannah was in my class. She was always just in front of me, a full head shorter, when we got in line. Her last name began with the letters B-a, just like mine.

   Hannah, I'm here,
   right behind you;
   I've released the rag of silence—
      (speak it!)
   this poem is your defense.

{Virginia Barrett lives in San Francisco, California. Born in New York City, New York. Poet & Artist. virginiabarrett.com}

Blood Cancer #1

They said it would do its will, have its way with her,
        as bullies often do.
They said, "It could change everything—even the rules of the game . . ."
        forgetting to finish the sentence, ". . .of life."
They also whispered, "There isn't much that can be done."
Endure. Stay upbeat. Hope. Pray. None of this, did they really expect
        to make any difference upon the outcome.
"The tyrant will return when it finds weakness," they whispered,
        ". . .as tormenters are wont to do."
"Bystander," they said, "Your job is to Go on Going On . . ."
They; the doctors, nurses, well-meaning family and friends,
        became part of the good fight.

The violence of its attack stunned each quiet witness.
She endured its theft of burly blood and vigor.
She stayed upbeat, taking their toxic onslaught
        upon each living, multiplying cell.
She hoped the torture would end before it finished her.
She learned to pray in the way of the Old Country,
        in an Ancient, Fervent Tongue.
She; no longer read "victim," no longer stood by,
        no longer merely took the blows.
The attacker; no longer the victor, lost interest,
        and abandoned its mission.

{Lior Jacober lives in Orinda, California. Born and raised in Cleveland,
  Ohio. Teacher & Nature Lover.}

Silent

As a little-fingered boy
beneath the spider-legged table
and its drapy lace, I believed
conking my rubber soldiers in their groins
could hurt a bad guy
real good,
but later, sitting up to the table
in the straight-back chair
and spooning pasty-pea soup out of a shallow bowl,
I held they were only playthings,
and never told
about my milk money and Brucie Powell.

{Mark Meierding lives in Rohnert Park, California. Born and raised in Meiners Oaks, California. Youthful & Aged.}

Much Too Full

The world is full of jealous mothers: some crazy, some not.

Nobody ever writes about them unless they're movie stars
and then it's okay because they are hot Electro-Gothic
and sinister and perky and fun, but **the real everyday jealous
mothers are hot Electro-Gothic and sinister and perky
and no fun and not only do they wish their children to be
not as good as they are or were or ever will be but infinitely,
pathetically worse and totally incompetent** and that wish
continues until the day the mother dies at 22 or 93
or whenever and usually the wish lives as long as each
"would-be" infinitely, pathetically worse and totally
incompetent child tries to live a life.

**Speaking confidentially the real everyday jealous
mother is happy to explain in a comforting voice:**

the sound of which makes the Devil do a perfect
sign of the cross with the tip of his hallowed tail

**"I'm not like that. My children really are infinitely,
pathetically worse and totally incompetent,
worse than I am or was or ever will be. It's true."**

{Marvin R. Hiemstra lives in San Francisco, California. Born and raised in Iowa. Poet & Delight Commentator. drollmarv.com}

Duplicity

Remember, never make friends
with the side of you that's slow
on the uptake, may drop trays of succotash
and Salisbury steak on the lunchroom floor.
That's the part of you to avoid, or snicker at,
like you did with friends in the cloakroom,
feeling queenly over the one girl
made entirely of slowness,
what Brian Kopcke called *retarded*.
Never nod or smile in recognition
at the part of you, like her, that trips
over words or walks alone.

If possible, stand above frailty
as you did in the covered walkway,
looking down on the playground
as she was thrown
onto the merry-go-round by the boy mob
and spun and spun, shirt ripped
as she tried to fly herself off
but was battered back.

All done in pantomime from your height,
enough of a dumb play to watch
and completely disown.

{Kate Peper lives in Fairfax, California. Born and raised in Edina, Minnesota. Poet & Painter. peperprojects.com}

Clearing Away Alder Leaves

Sometimes in slow pools of Eshom creek
I twig away alder leaves
And see dark granite pebbles,
Minnows flashing into deeper water,
Water that runs deep and dark
Into a valley far below;
I see a tilled field by a pasture,
A father and two small boys.
The bigger boy hits and throws
The smaller boy onto the clods.
The father unglues and rages:
"You little son-of-a-bitch!
Don't you ever hit your little brother;"
Then he picks up and throws
The bad boy onto the clods.
The boy is crying loud
And wets his pants in fear.
The father screams, "You're too
Goddamn old to be wetting your pants:
How old are you? You're seven years old,
Too old to be pissing your pants;
You know what I'm going to do
When we are through working on this fence?
We are going to the house,
And I'm going to cut your peter off;
You'll squat like a girl to pee;
You won't need a peter for that anymore.
Stop your goddamn crying
And feeling sorry for yourself,
Get up and get to work
Before I spank you again."

The little boy sniffles,
Quickly swallows the lumps in his throat,
Grabs his groin through his wet
Denim pants and jumps up;
Dreading to work, fearing to go home,
Knowing there is no place to go,
He helps his father mend a broken fence.
And this sometimes I see
Clearing away alder leaves
In quiet dark pools of Eshom creek
In a valley far below.

Another Remedy

She gives my daughter an hour's therapy
and her old New Yorkers;
she tells me my daughter is not crazy—
but suicidal with low self-esteem—
that it will take a long time
to get through this stage,
but together we can traverse
the paths of this period
hopefully without major falls;
"we are like training wheels," she says.

I thank her with twenty;
she smiles and hands me
May 1997 *New Yorker;*
I read where Mrs. Eden
has come to town carrying
coyote piss; (She can scare off deer
with it.) she even ponders using
human hair and pissing in a jar
as alternatives to ridding
the demon deer; I think
how easy her measures are
to correcting the unwanted deer—
they exist, but are kept away.
How could I do this?

{Bill Simmons lives in Carroll, Iowa. Born in Kingsburg, California and
raised in the central valley.}

Hardly Lord Jim

I was the one
who got on all fours
behind chubby
and unsuspecting Fred
when Mike
shoved him in the chest
and he fell backward
over me
while Donny laughed.

That was it, as I remember.
Nobody went to the hospital.
There was no blood.
The grass
absorbed the fall,
most likely.

So
here I am
at the other end
of my life,
hardly Lord Jim,
but still
unable to put out
of my mind
me there
on all fours.

{Roy Mash lives in San Rafael, California. Born and raised in Detroit, Michigan. Cursed & Carefree. roymash.com}

Black Flowers

Faces sunscorched   fists tight
as knots   they surround him
in his backyard.
    Knuckles

fly like bats   dust and
blood.
    Shame

births black flowers
he'll be rid of
    as soon as he

forgets
    those hands
    those faces

{David Beckman lives in Santa Rosa, California. Born and raised in Jamestown, New York. Poet & Playwright.}

Childhood

My name was Lucille Lang then,
and oh, how I hated it!
The other children called me Lois Lane,
Blue Seal Langendorf and Lou the Seal.
Sometimes they called me Chinesey
because Lang rhymes with Wang and Tang.

I wanted to wake up on another planet
where I could skip through fall leaves
tumbling along the sidewalk
and watch rain glitter as it hit the slick street
without ducking dirt clods thrown
by boys from Egbert W. Beach School.

I wanted to grow up quickly
and look like Brigitte Bardot, even though
my father took me to the movies on Saturdays,
and my mother always let me
lick dough off the beaters
when we baked chocolate chip cookies.

I wanted to be big enough to outrun
Mike and Rusty. I grew faster
and reached this milestone at ten. I craved
popularity with the other kids,
but I was chosen last, or nearly last,
for the kickball teams, again and again.

But none of this matters anymore.
Lucille is from the Latin, meaning "light."
Lang is German for "long." I learned to smile
at the sound of these syllables:
long light. It traverses darkness.
It fuels the rain forest. It's forged by the stars.

{Lucille Lang Day lives in Oakland, California. Born and raised in
Piedmont, California. Poet & Author.}

Concerning your story about the man who kept the praises in his wallet:

I thought that you were going to say that instead of praising him the students were so brazen that they vilified him. If they had been hateful, and the teacher nevertheless gave the student the paper, he still might have kept it in his wallet and with just as much poignancy because, either way, it's the cherishing of that paper that is testament to the old wound.

When I was a kid, I pulled the wings off butterflies, squashed the abdomens of fireflies in order to make glowing rings, and threw grasshoppers into fires....

Sometimes, the grasshopper's bodies would make a sound as they exploded. Often, I would turn my head because the sound of the grasshopper's death was to intimate to my own mortality. I turned away, too, in order to continue these acts that were anathema to my conscience. I insisted.

And here's a nice story: When my friend was in first grade at a Quaker elementary school, another pupil was stealing finger paintings. My friend suggested to his teacher that they hide in the cloakroom to catch the thief. His teacher said, "Why don't you paint two paintings?" – you can enjoy making both and keep one for yourself, and let him have the other." Forty years after I heard the story, the teacher's message finally hit me: Don't covet even what you think is your own. Wow!

Patty

Her last name was Lucas and we
exercised our poetic ignorance
with the likes of Mucas, Pucas, and
worse, each day a new verse
of torment for a girl born poor.
I ride that bus over and over in my
cell, where, for sixteen years I've
thrown spitballs and gum at a
little girl who never cried.
And I cry.
I weep with a Karma Chameleon that
is my muse, my Virgil, my guide
back to a place where Patty is
precious and her feet are mine
to wash.

{James Oliver Dempsey lives in Bayboro, North Carolina. Born and
raised in Camden, New Jersey. Poet & Artisan.}

To the Editor: Dear Joe,

Name hazing began in second grade. I was new to this school. I didn't know anyone, but I soon became the champion of the boys at marbles, with my great grandmother's cache of ancient cat eyes, stone "boulders," steelies in two sized, agates and crystal puries. She sewed me a draw-string bag for them on her treadle sewing machine—big enough for the marbles I'd win. And win I did. When my bag got too full, I gave back the winnings—glass marbles you could buy at the store—but never my treasure.

Grandmother's gift helped me connect to my new world as it had her own little boy in 1918. These were Uncle Grant's marbles. But I was a kid in 1954 and I had to test the boundaries in my new world.   I am still haunted by calling out in the noon line, "Sara Salvato the big potato." The beautiful Miss Ready brought me into line in the moment, saying, "Why Julia, I'm surprised at you, that's unkind." Her face, which I worshiped, clouded with hurt. Her goodness and voice conveyed a disappointment with me that has made all the difference in that being nipped in the bud. What a beautiful day it is.

Intimations of Quan Yin

Dear Sisters & Brothers of any form of extreme loss or violence,

I thank you for being agents of love, kindness, intelligence and forgiveness on my life journey. It is your clarity or vivid struggle, or such, from your childhood heritage, that has shaped the contours of my dark cave walk to the Source of Inner Guidance, which is the inner temple where God lives within me and keeps whispering, "live, love, forgive, and know joy, for surely this living force of all good Is 'the force that through the green fuse drives the flower.'"

I am so grateful to you, Radiant Angels, every one! For deep within the core fire of your soul, you hammered and fashioned an exquisite tiller to right the vulnerable and fragile sailboat of your life, to stay the course of dignity and decency to heal the world's remembered history, and life by life, yours' included, to grow the human hope that is the Wholeness and Unity that Is the One, born in the infancy of all of us, the One that loves us unconditionally, until we finally open our evolved eye to see It.

All my love, Julia

{Julia Vose lives in Sebastopol, California. Born in Jacksonville, Florida, raised in Bakersfield, San Mateo and Modesto, CA. Poet & Novelist.}

the earth remembered me

the evening grosbeaks came
held tenderly in a sea of birds

mud carried seeds in its pockets
sunflowers

I slept as never before
nothing between me but grey birds with yellow foreheads

if you had said just let the birds do their work in the darkness

if you had said there is a way to be happy

felt the earth's hand on my forehead
felt the birds skitter over my body

pecking for sunflower seeds

We are talking bullies

sometimes a weed is   when it turns into stickers
sometimes a wisteria when as a snake it strangles the birch
sometimes I'm a bully when I go to the dump in the rain
and it will make you cold

sometimes the day bullies
I am a bully when I sit on you
to be peaceful you have to be a rock

you knew how to contain graywackle and mantle
you have connections to the stone in the center

so when I sit on you I can be quiet
it takes the bully out of me knowing what my backyard is made of
Indian pipestone and the hands of pepperweed

it takes the bully out of you when you think you're intruding
and I call you sweetheartfleshbonessunset

{Catherine Ferguson lives in Galisteo, New Mexico. Born in Mexico City
and raised in Scottsdale, Arizona. Poet & Painter.}

Minor Accident, End of Term, Spring 1970

Dorm-porch college boys,
third-rate mech-tech school,
laughing at the kid
who lost it down the hill,
smashed bike, head over curb
into a wind-break tree.

Not one comes down to help.
Kid grips shattered bike,
drags it back home.

River of blood coursing down
the kid's t-shirt, a growing red
flower, flag of the sixties,
summer of love
and all that—

Wouldn't come out in the wash,
so the kid's mom throws
it in the trash can downstairs.

{Tony Reevy lives in Durham, North Carolina. Poet & Father.
tonyreevy.com}

Again

Mom and Dad are both alive.
Mom, still clear-minded, cooks dinner every night,
manages a sweet smile when I come in.
Dad sits at the table waiting to be served,
but my brother's the one in charge, the crazy
are always in charge, it's dangerous
to cross them, one jab of a clown elbow
and they're lost, or ruin everything.

At night I walk down the street past the communist's
bleak stucco house spiky with palm trees, past
the blue cottage where the lady had a nervous breakdown:
dark rooms, afghans. What's a nervous breakdown, Mama?
Halloween, we were scared to ring the doorbells
on their unlit porches—this was the fifties,
before my brother was first shackled,
before I had kids of my own.

Now a young man comes toward me in a fancy restaurant,
letting in a cold wind. I recognize him,
handsome as De Niro in his dark suit,
but the strange light in his eyes can only mean one thing.
I tell myself this isn't happening, I belong somewhere else.
His shoulders are coated with big wet leaves.
They hang down his arms like a loose cape
and scatter over the tables as he heads straight for me.

{Linda Lancione lives in Berkeley, California. Born in Oakland,
California, raised in the East Bay. Poet & Storyteller.}

Nowhere Fast

Pointed out to me, he looked as tall
as any grown man—but really he was just
a skinny high school boy from our neighborhood.
The thing about him was his nose—the reason why
the others called him Profile.

My mind's eye, six decades on, shows me
a big blade on a face I wouldn't know
if I met him in on my street. We didn't know
anything about him or his family, except
our older brother and our cousin said
he beat up on little kids. His nickname
in my brother's mouth came out public and rough,
as if toilet-stall graffiti spoke out loud—
Here I sit broken-hearted...

That left a smear of dread in me,
to picture that boy cornered
by my muscled brother and my cousin.
Anything Rick said, I took as gospel,
so when he told me Profile was a bad one
I knew it would come to blood.

You had to think he had it coming.
We knew that meant they'd fix him,
teach him a lesson.
When I thought about it
I got that feeling in my gut,
that sick scared flutter
of no way out, as if it were me

backed up, without an ally
in the nightmare corner
where your legs spin
like jelly wheels,
taking you nowhere fast.

I tried to figure out
what that lesson was
they had to teach him
and how it would fix
that tall skinny boy
inside, where he was broken.

{Calvin Ahlgren lives in San Rafael, California. Tennessee-born.
Gardener & Tai Chi Teacher.}

Tact Can Be a Weapon
That Declaws Opponents

Anger causes our backs to arch,
the fur along our spines and tails
to form a ridge,
making us seem larger,
more menacing.

I want to draw back my upper lip,
snarl and wrinkle my face as I
hiss and spit.

After testing my claws,
verifying their sharpness,
my anger toward
the hissing of others
is muted.

Some, ready to pounce,
see my head bent low
as I approach,
weaving a bit left and right—
they decide to play.

{Jane Herschlag lives in Danbury, Connecticut. Poet/Photographer &
Nature Lover. arbyherschlag.com photographyjane.com}

To the editor or to whom it may concern:

I consider myself socially liberal and fiscally conservative. I have to take issue with your Bullies & Bystanders Project. Do you really believe that coddling our children, shielding them from the realities of life will be beneficial to them? If they don't learn that sticks and stones may break their bones and that words will never harm them, if they don't learn that one must fight back to succeed, they're in for a shocker when they have to compete with the people of other nations who will not take prisoners. I'm a retired autoworker, a union man through and through, and I know fighters win, wimps lose. The weaklings need to be toughened up and/or weeded out. This country is getting soft and publications like the one you're proposing will weaken us even further if successful. Our position in the world as a leader for democracy and decency is being threatened. There are tigers at the gate and they *are* barbarians! If you have the courage to print this letter I'll sign it:

Bully for You!

{Teddy McLaren lives in Chicago, Illinois. Born and raised in Michigan. Veteran & Voter.}

Assembling the Bench Press

My son says this'll be a cinch.
He's 15 and says we follow the pictures.
I'm 46 and say we follow the words.
It has 87 parts and they all have names.
I find this reassuring as he hands me
a carriage bolt, an aircraft nut, a washer
as I lie on my back with an adjustable wrench
and pliers, and tell him the story of when I was
15 and walking home from school across
Taylor Park, minding my own business
when Nicky Vespa and Kenny Hovanek
and a red-headed girl whose name I think was Frankie
stopped me in the no man's land between
two baseball fields, for directions.
Nicky knocked my books down and directed
me to pick them up, then Kenny slapped me
hard in the face, then the girl looked
away. Then we all waited to see what
I would do. I got myself a bench press
from Sears and Roebuck. I was 15 and
motivated. Arnold Schwarzenegger was
undiscovered and bodybuilding in Austria.
My son quietly hands me the lat bar frame
and axle bushing. The only sound's the turn
of the screw, and me grunting underneath
the evolving machine. "But what did you
do? when he hit you?" he needs to know.

But in that moment, the moment
that got me started counting sets of reps,
thousands of reps in my basement night after night
gritting my teeth and trembling underneath
the oppressive weight of those two ghosts
and that red head still looking away—in that
moment that counted—I only fought back
the tears. Unsuccessfully. I line
up the pivot, secure it with a hex bolt, lie:
"It was 30 years ago, how should I
remember?"

{Paul Hostovsky lives in Boston, Massachusetts. Born and raised in New Jersey. Poet & ASL Interpreter. paulhostovsky.com}

Of Boys and Men

Home from camp all flushed and angry
the son says he tried to stop
boys from torturing frogs, begged
his counselor to make them stop
but the man said, "Boys will be boys."

His father tells him a childhood story
about stopping kids from throwing stones
at a cat tied to a post.
They talk about the pain
of cats and frogs and boys.

When they take a walk after dinner
they're careful to step over worms
that surfaced after rain.

{Patti Tana lives on Long Island, New York. Grew up in the Hudson
River Valley. Poet & Teacher. pattitana.com}

Male Violence

Boys in tee shirts and cutoffs laugh and make mudballs
at the edge of Cedar Lake then throw them at ducks
and mallards close to shore, like they will throw snowballs
soon , like they may have last week, when an inch or two
fell, their hands cupping and patting with the eager
hope of whom or what they might aim at, fire, and hit.

mud-and-nettle at the edge of Carmel River
School's playground the oaks and ferns along the river
and lagoon provided cover for stealth and war
at recess I jumped Jeff from behind pushed him to
the ground headlocked him yelled had enough give give he'd
muttered yeah get off me you son of a bitch I
let him up ashamed and proud ran to nettles threw
clods and mudballs at each other until the bell
rang for the return to classes

Rooted in the old ammunition of insult,
a boy's innocent smile leads so easily to
the silent mask of grim teeth clenching four-letter
words, neck twisted, waiting for a bell, spring, autumn,
a sign that may not come in time: aim, fire, then hit.

{Brian Cronwall lives on the island of Kaua'i, Hawai'i. Born in
San Francisco and raised in Carmel, California. Teacher & Poet.}

Pablo

Ma had me confess too much, Doc,
whipped my ass when I skipped school
      ever since I was nothin' but a kid.

I was a set-up for Ralphie
from as early as who knows when.
I'd tail Ralphie 'round the block.
He'd knock me around
      but I was real tough.
He was already in and out of Juvie.

Ma made me see our priest
and I seen a La Cura, our local healer,
      who got bad spirits off my back.
But I was already on the corner,
learning the ropes:
      never cross Mariposa,
      no red gear at night.

I watched the big boys fight it out.
Got hi-signed with flying colors,
      bloodied a jerk in blue.

Kept arms length from crack
      as I seen Ralphie waste away.
Nice guy who hated himself so bad.

Ma brought me in here for clap
      and shit she thought I caught.
But I never shot up and never did it
      without a damn condom.
She'd head off to her room at night
      and cry like a baby.

Got myself into Juvie twice
        and when I got out, man,
was I cool in the 'hood.

Robertito started tailing me
before I almost got myself killed
in a hell-of-a-shoot-out.

I took off to Tia Rosa's in Oakland.
Thought I'd come back over the bridge today
        to see you, Doc.

Do you burn off tattoos?
This one pegs me on the street
        so I wear my jacket night and day.

Does it hurt?

That Stone

That stone
grey on the ground
can be lifted
it can be thrown
to hit the flesh
and bruise it
blue

That stick
can be taken hold of
lifted to smack
down upon the body
with its sting
and smart

While words
roil in the throat
they can be spat out
to char the mind
flamed
into the face

burn
into the heart
sear the soul
brand deep
a scar
into the unprotected
spirit

{Richard Cruwys Brown lives in Kentfield, California. Born and raised in Minneapolis, Minnesota. Country-boy & City-boy.}

Motherfucker

They say the underdog eventually wins,
but I haven't found the *they* to verify their sources.
It's tough to take the bull out of a bully
and beware of the ram when your back is turned.
A stretch for me to forgive ignorance,
but unfettered meanness even harder.

The biggest bully I know told me
this is who I am. That's the apology,
as if she were powerless to change.
Attributes hostility to others. Hires lawyers
to intimidate. A runaway train that takes pride
in disrespect. Addicted to power,
she abuses even her infirm mother.
At 500 miles away, this in-law is too close to home.
Does she feel stillness in the woods? Peace at dawn?

Her tormenting gives shadow a bad name.
I am exploring how to take a stand
before empathy and compassion exhaust me.
I no longer care how intimidating
or dictatorial her father was.
Turn the other cheek is taking on
a below-waist nuance closer
to a bare moon.
Don't mistake it for a bow.

{Sandy Scull lives in Forest Knolls, California. Born and raised in Byrn
Mawr, Pennsylvania. Dancer & Weed Puller.}

The Fair Fight

Walking to the cafeteria
I hear it—almost inarticulate—
like the shouts of a primitive clan
killing a mammoth,
Get him!, Come on, Alfie!
Don't be chicken!

I see students running
toward a circle in the quad.
By the time I get there
a sizeable crowd has gathered
in the midst of which
two big, muscular youths
punch, gouge, kick,
wrestle on the ground.

One's Alfie, my ex-student;
the other's named Armand.
I try to penetrate the circle
shouting, *Stop! I'm a teacher!*
as we're expected to do,
but two of Armand's gang
lock arms in front of me,
all the while screaming,
Kick him, Armand! Fuck him up!

Both boys are bleeding
when two burly teachers
and a campus security guard
break through the circle,
take them away.
The crowd disperses
debating about who won.

Later that day, Victor,
a polite boy in my class
whom I'd never have suspected
to be cruel, remarks,
It was an okay fight
but I like it better
when it's two on one.

Leadership Potential

He sets off a stink bomb in class, calls the boy delivering the bulletin *Eraserhead*, harasses a girl till she rushes out crying, steals from my cabinet, won't sit down, gives the finger to an aide outside the window, flashes sunlight with a mirror into everyone's eyes, brags he's been suspended twenty-one times from his last high school.

I call his mother. Thrice divorced, she exclaims, *He comes from a stable family!* I talk to his counselor. He replies, *He's really a nice boy, intelligent, and a good athlete too; he has leadership potential.* Finally, like a supplicant going to Buddha to beg for a miracle, I approach an assistant principal. He talks with the boy and tells me, *He says he didn't do the things you said, but he's sorry he upset you. He's promised to apologize.*

He leads my class in open rebellion. Students refuse to move from the window when there's a fight outside. One screams out, *Don't you touch me!* when I put my fingers lightly on his shoulder. I find gang symbols and a host of insults written on the desks. The boy continues to disrupt as if he has a mission.

I hear him urging the class bully to beat up a weaker boy. He writes on his desk, *Don't be shy and don't be nervous. Come to Laue's blowjob service.* I send a note to another vice principal: *Why isn't he out of school?* When I next encounter her, she shouts, *Are you implying we're not doing our jobs?* I answer as diplomatically as I can.

Finally she says, *I'll check on him with other teachers.* A week later he's transferred to continuation school. I tell my wife, *I've just gotten free of a student who's handsome, talented, intelligent, and who ruined my class all by himself. In ten years of teaching, I'd never seen the like of him. He reminds me of the leader in Lord of the Flies?*

{John Laue lives in La Selva Beach, California. Born in Easton, Pennsylvania, raised in Wanaque and Belvidere, N.J. Teacher & Poet.}

Shame

I can't recall what word or slight enraged me
at recess when I grabbed your boney wrist
and swung you round like a rag doll,
then thud and whimper as you hit the ground.

Got his ass kicked by a girl!
It was a jeer no bully could resist.

Predatory boys gave you swirlies in the bathroom.
In the lunch line they'd yell in your face
Hey, Chester [fingers stabbing your chest]
glad to see you back [slapping homo on your back]
as you struggled not to fall.

Your delicate mother, milk-faced and nervous,
brought cupcakes for everyone on your birthday.
How could she have known
how much worse that bribe made your days?
Mama's boy, they hissed on the playground, pussy.

That last time you came back from bathroom break,
hair dripping on your button down shirt,
near-hysterical, crying, hiccoughing so hard,
the teacher had to take you outside to calm you.

The boys snorted and laughed,
then looked at their shoes, fidgeted,
squirmed in their seats like small animals
caught in traps.

{June Sylvester Saraceno lives in Truckee, California. Born and raised in
Elizabeth City, North Carolina. Poet & Professor. junesaraceno.com}

Fifty Years of Change

Fifty years ago, when I was in high school, the word "bullying" was almost never used. We knew the term "assault and battery." Social Darwinism was definitely the rule of the day. My high school was all-male, in the hierarchy of upper and lower classmen was to be respected and preserved. We called the teachers Mr., and they replied in kind, using only our last names. The same convention was to be applied between upper and lower classmen. Physical assault was not allowed but embarrassment, ridicule, and some degree of physical contact was not only allow, but expected. It was the duty of the upperclassman to demand "respect", and the obligation of the lower-classmen to test the convention. Some individuals managed this delicate balance better than others. The underlying concept then was that we would be graduating into a highly competitive world where psychological and physical toughness would be required.

I believed, then, wholeheartedly in the "concept," and that no upperclassman would dare to do actual, permanent physical harm. I had no thought of psychological damage to myself or others.

I confess now, that I was essentially unconscious, and probably uncaring, regarding the plight of most of my classmates. The so-called "concept" was also supported by my family and the culture in which I lived. I had every reason to believe that these high school years of "testing" were central to my potential achievement in the future. In addition, my worldview was highly myopic and I wasted little time thinking about the welfare of others. Of course, this is no longer true in me, and I believe in growing numbers of individuals in our culture. All too many misdeeds are the result of unconsciousness and/or ignorance. Happily, the efforts of many have brought the light of awareness to this issue.

Fifty years has brought important and welcome changes in attitude and behavior.

In addition, attention to, and criticism of "bully-ism" today has made it almost impossible for children of middle and high school age to be unaware of the devastating effect hazing and humiliation can have on many individuals.

{Author lives in San Rafael, California. Born and raised in St. Louis, Missouri. Student & Teacher.}

Somewhere along the road, we have all been bullied in one way or another, some worse than others. Terrorists are really bullies with guns. Bullying can be verbal or physical and how we deal with all of it is perhaps our clue to survival.

The tragedy of human existence
Is that we
Are all so vulnerable.

{Rebecca Young Winslow lives in Petaluma, California. Born in Tippecanoe, Ohio, at age ten moved to San Francisco. Creative & Fun.}

Angry on the Phone

banks hands on your money
may sometimes cling
well what i mean is im in venice and zip
my wall money wont come
walking back towards a phone i rehearse
indignation exasperation patience guile
what do you mean i cant etc
and how many years you ask
more than youve been born sweetie
but then its all fixed the rain stops mail arrives
lets get a nap before lunch

14 september 06

{Patrick Smith lived in San Francisco, California. Born in Menominee, Michigan. Poet & Artist & a Wallace Stevens' maven. pancakepress.com}

The Bad Boy

We are here, on David's petite lawn,
the exotic tree at one corner of the lot,
a tree from fairytale, not eight feet tall,
thick with crêpe paper leaves hanging to the ground,
the interior hidden.

Once David strung a wire across the street,
waited in the bushes like a patient hunter.
When Kenny Wells came barreling past on his bike,
David pulled the wire taut, caught Kenny by the throat
and lifted him clean off his seat and hard to the road.

That's just one story; there are more to tell.
Today we are drawn by the rumor, the danger of a knife.
David's brother is here, the sweet, younger brother.
My sister is here, the Cozarts, Dave Antill.
When a stranger speeds by in his long, blue sedan,

David lets the knife fly, into the car, past the driver's nose,
thwack in the passenger seat. Wheels screech.
The car backs slowly. "Who threw this?" he demands,
climbing out of the car, knife in hand. We are statues.
We look toward the tiny house because, of course,

David is gone. Our voices, we never had.
Mrs. Ianni, the fat Italian mother, is rousted from inside,
her Italianness exotic in this neighborhood.
She props the screen door ajar, her hip a placeholder,
as the man shows her the knife, gesticulates

with his other hand, insists deeply.
She steps off the porch, crosses the steamy lawn
to her other son, her good son. She slaps his head and we gasp.
Over her shoulder, to the stranger, "He's a bad boy. His knife."

Leaves rustle.

{Cathy Barber lives in San Mateo, California. Raised in the Cleveland, Ohio area. Teacher & Poet. cathy-barber.net}

Unicorns

She climbs into the car
and makes me swear I will not tell:
those two girls with yellow hair
and pink barrettes
are really unicorns.
They only visit the first grade
spying upon the human world.

The plastic crowns with tassels
that they wear to school are proof.
Of course she may not wear one.
She's lucky they let an ordinary girl
into the club.
At night they head back to the woods
and dance among the trees
while she's asleep in bed.
It's true she says.
She eyes me savagely
and turns away.

Once home she slips into my room
and sneaks out the page
of gold and silver stars
I've saved to chart her good behavior.
She cuts out a paper crown
and glues these jewels around the edge,
parading the crown
she will not wear to school.
She marches past me to the mirror
and I surrender all the stars
to my cold silent child
who makes her way alone
in the new order.

{Jill Stein lives in Princeton, New Jersey. Born and raised in Brooklyn,
New York. Poet & Psychotherapist.}

Jeremy

His name was Jeremy
Since the day of his birth, his name was always Jeremy
until he came to school and his name changed for him
Yeah... Jeremy he was the kid that I never talked to
The kid that I didn't notice until the day
I heard his name over the loudspeaker
and read it in the newspaper
He was quiet
I never thought much of him except that he was just another emo
pill-popper
I never knew
I could never know or understand how it could get so bad
or how you could not love yourself even the slightest bit
I should have known
Everyone should have known
He didn't believe in the promise of it gets better
He would look to the stars and see nothing but darkness
He would listen to a song and hear nothing but emptiness
He would look at the colors and see nothing but black and white
He was alone in a world that told him you need friends
You need someone to find
you cool
Darkness would hang over him like a dying tree
Soon he would become the tree himself
He would wish and hope for something
A sign?
A little bit of wisdom?
So here I am trying to give you or anyone out there a sign that says
It Gets Better

{Paivi Miller is an 8th Grade student at Saint Philip's Elementary School,
San Francisco, California}

Bystanders

On the school playground,
the two combatants in the middle,
wrestling on the blacktop,
backpacks tossed to the side,
no sound from the two fighters
pulling hair, jabbing fists,
rolling over,
cheered on by the spectators
who make no move to stop
this violence,
like viewers of a TV program,
watching,
forgetting this is real life—

not something staged.

{Nancy Haskett lives in Modesto, California. Born and raised in Long Beach, California. Poet & Reader.}

The Bully's Journey

Steelboy, scourge of the local schoolyard
slung dirtballs packed with stones
to extend his range of terror
beyond the reach of his angry fists

a story was told of his rage
and how the younger fellows' heads
reacted to the concrete
during playground poundings

but when adults were asked for advice
most spoke favorably of Steelboy's
independence and leadership
and it was very discouraging

so I approached him one day to ask
why his name was Steelboy
thinking friendship was safer
than victimization

not fooled, Steelboy took a swing
at my nose and missed by a hair
then howled in misery
frustrated that he couldn't connect

years later I wonder what became
of Steelboy, thinking that it must
have been difficult for him
to live such a life, never satisfied

checking online, asking around town
it appears Steelboy didn't last for long;
fearing enemies—the stress of anger—
kills

{Bobby Coleman lives in San Francisco, CA. Born and raised in
N. Merrick and Bellmore, NY. Poet & Humanist. WeAreAllPoets.com}

The Happy Man

for Rustin Larson

I see him the shark fisherman
a big-bear-of-a-man when I shop at the store

he speaks Spanish with a plump dapper man
who was in line with me at the bank

this castaway lost from December 2012
from Mexico landing more then 6,000 miles away on Ebon

his 25-foot-long boat covered in gooseneck barnacles
his teen companion vomited raw meat and died

the man, Jose Salvador Alvarenga,
has a daughter, Fatima, in El Salvador

lived in Mexico as an illegal immigrant
this man landed on January 30, 2014

thirteen months catching turtles with his bare hands
drinking his own urine catching rainwater

I'm oblivious at Island Pride ear infections
grieving a death in the family mad sad mad again

I handle the Fuji apples I hear Spanish
see the big bear and the smaller plump man

then in line at the store they're behind me
I wave to Yukiko her husband kids

just as well I'm woozy I buy a paper
what a strange trip it's been

when I leave the store the happy man
the beaming big man is still there

only later do I figure out
I've imagined the happiest man I'll ever meet

The Flashback

An annoyance more than anything
a fly buzzing by my face

It's nothing really
only an echo nearly fifty years ago

Only a boy walking down the street
shoots me in the head when I walk by

his eyes cold and fierce
only a small Marshallese boy

It's only a game
I once shot water pistols in Arizona

and yet the echo slaps me
like that memory of the return boat trip from Arno

the huge waves wash over me
I hang onto the boat rail getting bruised

only once in Phoenix I faced a gun
same age as the small boy glaring at me

only a girl manning the register
see my father's arm over my head

my father grabs the gun from the gunman
his finger bleeds

my father waves the revolver
says this is my store

only one memory out of many
in over fifty years of living

my father is long dead
why can't I forget

{Paula Yup lives in Spokane, Washington. Born and raised in Phoenix, Arizona. Writer & Drawer.}

Dodgeball

Trapped in the outer circle with white balls
Whizzing in all directions, children shrieked
And laughed, and most were soon hit and retired
Gladly, and told the circle how to throw.
Four lasted a while, then suddenly stood still
Deliberately, obedient to a rule
The teacher sensed but could not specify.
Then once again (she should have known) that girl
Who always became the target spun and crouched
Alone, and the eyes of children grew so hard
It seemed some primitive, horrific rite
Was taking place. Harder and faster they threw,
Yet could not tag her. Time stood still. The sweat
Poured from her body, and that haunted look
Came over her, as of a sacrifice
Long dreaded. Finally, about to intervene,
The teacher heard the bell, and said "Okay,
Let's have the balls." A snarl or whine broke out,
And as the girl retired and relaxed,
A white ball flew and hit her on the back.
And so she turned, and stared upon them all
With such contempt it made the teacher shiver,
And handed her the ball, and stalked away
To classes which, compared to this, were play.

{B.E. Stock lives in Brooklyn, New York. Born in New York City, raised in Connecticut. Poet & Godlover.}

Harm

I wonder if I did you harm then—
back when we were young, you so fragile

—to suggest, in fact implore you
to believe that reality actually could be

you and me against or amidst the world
as if nothing or no one else actually mattered

when, afterwards, for the great bulk of it,
I, no longer being part of us,

you managed to be your lost and losing
self alone against an insuperable foe.

Now that you've lost the battle and your wits,
I need your losses to afford you perfect release.

Creating the Furniture

To straighten her out,
they *nailed* her feet and hands
to the table or was it
held her hands and feet
to the table in order to
beat her good or as Daddy said
to *ruin* her while Mommy
held her down? Or was it
their caring for her that she
would stop the hanging out
at Feller's Drugstore or
did they want to build a new couch
with Frank's sister to cushion it,
to *sit* on her? And where was Frank
sitting by at the time and why?
Actually he'd preferred his standing.

{Ed Coletti lives in Santa Rosa, California. Born in the Bronx, raised on
Long Island, NY. Poet & Artist. edwardcolettispoetryblog.blogspot.com}

An Impression

If I say I'm sorry will you return?
I can do you greater justice.
Forgive me.
Watch as I prostrate myself for your enjoyment
nose to earth
prepared to taste your wrath directly.
Do I sense the great Ha?

She intended to stay still indefinitely
hoping that paralysis was the better stance,
acceptable.
She wondered whether fatigue was punishable by death.

audible sigh

h	o
e	I
w	l
a	i
n	v
t	e
s	o
n	n
o	t
o	h
n	e
e	m
t	e
o	d
t	i
o	a
u	n
c	s
h	t
m	r
e	i
s	p

{Ellen Litwack lives in Los Angeles.}

The Rodeo

The Mariposa County Fair is a small affair
tucked into the Sierra Nevada mountains
where my mother lives. This year I take
my young son with his grandma in hand
to gallivant along the crowded paths
past lemonade and popcorn,
ribboned whirly-gigs, festooned baseball caps,
toward the wooden stands of the rodeo.
Metal loudspeakers hung from the rafters
ask us to stand for the pledge of allegiance
as ragged old men with cowboy hats
and cherub-faced little boys with pointy boots
all rise for the blond high school girl singing
as though the Iraq war depends on every note.
After a robust blessing for all the young men
still defending our country in the desert
where the Bible was born,
we settle again on our wooden benches
and began to cheer for the brave cowboys
shot with a Hiyaah! from their chutes
toward the defenseless calves running
wild-eyed towards non-existing cover.

My son sits quiet, till one rambunctious calf
manages to evade the lasso as the horn sounds.
The dusty cowboy curses his failure,
a hundred men sink to their seats—
but my son, enthralled, hops up and down
clapping for the four-legged rebel
snorting his way past the flailing clown
back to his own kind.

{Dane Cervine lives in Santa Cruz, California. Born and raised in
Atwater, California. Poet & Therapist. DaneCervine.typepad.com}

Running River

The hands of a clock slowly moves forward
Scratching deep wounds into our sorrowful souls
The fear we feel and the pain we experience
Life is like a flowing river
Manipulated by the selfish moon
Yet it is always flowing
Always changing
Always meeting the same inevitable end
Running into the vast ocean that is
Always full of opportunities and promise
Even though the trail might be hard
Full of many turns
Painful waterfalls
And many selfish people
There is always a calm ocean to comfort you

{Kimiko Shiro is in the 11th Grade at Tamalpais High School, Mill Valley, California.}

Acknowledgments

"Charlie Howard's Descent," from *Turtle Swan* by Mark Doty. Reprinted by permission of David R. Godine, Publisher, Inc. Copyright © 1987 by Mark Doty.

"Perfect Target," first published in the *Red Rock Review*, then in *Dark Card, Texas Review Press*. Copyright © 2009 by Rebecca Foust.

"Identity," from *Given Sugar, Given Salt*. NY: HarperCollins, 2001, used by permission of Jane Hirshfield, all rights reserved.

"Hardly Lord Jim," first published in *The Sow's Ear*, then in *Buyer's Remorse*. Reprinted by permission *Cherry Grove Press*. Copyright © 2014 by Roy Mash.

"The Ropes," published in *Renewing the Vows, David Robert Books*. Copyright © 2007 by Peter Schmitt. "Fat Kid," published in *Magnolia 3*. Copyright © 2010 by Peter Schmitt.

"Evacuation Day, June 5, 1942," published in *Complex Allegiances Anthology*, 2012 by *Wising Up Press*. Copyright © 2012 Jodi L. Hottel.

"Assembling the Bench Press," published in *Bending the Notes* 2008 by *Main Street Rag*, Copyright © 2008 by Paul Hostovsky.

"The Bad Boy," published in *Slant* 2014. Copyright © 2014 Cathy Barber.

"Cul-de-sac" and "To Ovidiu, Whose Voice I Still Don't Remember," published by *Alice James Books* 2010. Copyright © 2010 by Mihaela Moscaliuc.

"Utopia," by Gigi Wyatt, published in *Marin Poetry Center* 2014 *High School Poetry Anthology*. Reprinted with permission of the Marin Poetry Center. Copyright © 2014 by Marin Poetry Center.

"Passages," published in *Gargoyle*. Copyright © 2013 by Noel Sloboda.

"Prosody," from *Money Money Money / Water Water Water*. Copyright © 2014 by Jane Mead. Reprinted with permission of The Permission Company, Inc., on behalf of *Alice James Books*, alicejamesbooks.org.

"Jupiter, Venus, and Mars..." and "They bussed us to the induction center..." from *Even So: New and Selected Poems*, published by *White Pine Press* 2012. Copyright © 2012 by Gary Young.

"Intent on Restoring Disorder," winner of the Nazim Hikmet Poetry Competition 2014. Copyright © 2014 by Les Bernstein.

The text face used throughout this book is ITC Mendoza Roman designed in 1991 by José Mendoza y Almeida, French designer, typographer and teacher. Mendoza says of his work that he "always tries to mix rigor and sensitivity, and the feeling of a hand's gesture to his designs." He is considered the "godfather" of French type design.

The cover font and title pages are set in Optima, designed by Hermann Zapf for the D. Stempel AG foundry, Frankfurt, Germany.